One Soldier's Story

One Soldier's Story

1939-1945

From the Fall of Hong Kong to the Defeat of Japan

George S. MacDonell

THE DUNDURN GROUP
TORONTO · OXFORD

Copy-editor: Charles Stuart
Design: Jennifer Scott
Printer: Transcontinental

National Library of Canada Cataloguing in Publication Data

MacDonell, George S.
  One soldier's story : from the fall of Hong Kong to the defeat of the Japanese / George S. MacDonell.

ISBN 1-55002-408-6

1. MacDonell, George S.   2. World War, 1939-1945--Personal narratives, Canadian.   3. World War, 1939-1945 — Campaigns — China — Hong Kong.   4. World War, 1939-1945 — Prisoners and prisons, Japanese.   5. Prisoners of war — Canada — Biography.   I. Title.

D811.M2513 2002   940.54'8171   C2002-905049-9

1   2   3   4   5   06   05   04   03   02

THE CANADA COUNCIL | LE CONSEIL DES ARTS
FOR THE ARTS | DU CANADA
SINCE 1957 | DEPUIS 1957

ONTARIO ARTS COUNCIL
CONSEIL DES ARTS DE L'ONTARIO

We acknowledge the support of the **Canada Council for the Arts** and the **Ontario Arts Council** for our publishing program. We also acknowledge the financial support of the **Government of Canada** through the **Book Publishing Industry Development Program** and **The Association for the Export of Canadian Books**, and the **Government of Ontario** through the **Ontario Book Publishers Tax Credit** program.

Care has been taken to trace the ownership of copyright material used in this book. The author and the publisher welcome any information enabling them to rectify any references or credit in subsequent editions.

J. Kirk Howard, President

Printed and bound in Canada.⊗
Printed on recycled paper.
www.dundurn.com

Dundurn Press	Dundurn Press	Dundurn Press
8 Market Street	73 Lime Walk	2250 Military Road
Suite 200	Headington, Oxford,	Tonawanda NY
Toronto, Ontario, Canada	England	U.S.A. 14150
M5E 1M6	OX3 7AD	

One Soldier's Story

Take these men for your example. Like them, remember that Prosperity can be only for the free. That freedom is the sure possession of those alone who have the courage to defend it.

Taken from Pericles' funeral oration to the Athenians, these words are inscribed on the Great War Memorial Wall of the Soldiers' Tower at the University of Toronto.

Table of Contents

Foreword

- It was a great honour to be asked to write a few comments for the foreword to George MacDonell's story of his wartime experience and, in particular, his moving account of Canada's courageous Hong Kong veterans from the perspective of a soldier who was there.

  During my career in the Canadian Forces, I did have some contact with the Hong Kong Veterans Association and in particular with the late Roger Cyr, who I came to know and to admire greatly. However, it was not until I became Deputy Minister of Veterans Affairs Canada that I really got to know many of the members of this wonderful Association and their story.

  Theirs is a story of tremendous courage, exceptional devotion to duty, and selfless sacrifice. It is a story of tremendous comradeship and endurance; it is a story of strong leadership and outstanding teamwork. It is a story of ordinary Canadians doing extraordinary deeds in incredibly daunting, frequently horrific circumstances. Most of all, it is a story about the resilience, strength and dignity of the Human Spirit — about *never* giving up and *never* being defeated.

One Soldier's Story is a story which needs to be told to all Canadians and perhaps never more so than now as Canada strives to understand and to come together to confront the unpredictable and troubling threats of the post-September 11, 2001 world in which we live.

George MacDonell has done a marvellous job of telling the inspiring story of Canada's Hong Kong veterans in a clear, compelling and compassionate manner. In doing so he made me just a little bit prouder to be a Canadian. This is a "must read" for anyone with an interest in people, in Canada, in our history, and what "Service Before Self" really means.

Vice-Admiral (retired) Larry Murray, CMM, CD
Deputy Minister
Veterans Affairs Canada

Preface

One Soldier's Story is an eyewitness account of the men of Canada's C Force, who fought and who gave their lives in the service of their country in the Battle of Hong Kong in December 1941. It also tells of their ordeal when, after the battle, they became prisoners of war of the Japanese for nearly four years, until their release at the end of the war with Japan in 1945.

These were the first Canadian soldiers committed to battle, and, as the survivors of the battle and the prison camps, they were the last ones to come home from World War II.

Against overwhelming odds, only partially trained and short of essential equipment, without thought of surrender they fought bravely for their beliefs in the best traditions of the Canadian Army. Their conduct both on and off the battlefield and in Japanese prison camps was characterized by their courage and their loyalty to their country.

Theirs is a story not of how they were defeated at Hong Kong but of how their spirit triumphed over desperate odds on the battlefield and over the slave labour, brutality, and starvation they experience in the prison camps.

I am pleased to commend this chapter of Canadian history to all Canadians and to contribute to the memory of this little-known story and those brave young men.

H. Clifford Chadderton, CC, OOnt, OStJ, CLJ, CAE, DCL, LLD
Patron, Hong Kong Veterans Association of Canada
Chairman, National Council of Veterans Association

Acknowledgements

My deep thanks must begin with Carl Vincent, who, through his outstanding book *No Reason Why*, contributed so much to an understanding of the Canadian involvement at Hong Kong in 1941. Through his research and analysis, Carl set out with accuracy the strategic, political, and geographic framework within which *One Soldier's Story* has been told. His assessment of British defence plans and his description of the overall battle of Hong Kong have been the most instructive and have stood the test of time. Not only was his book of great help in explaining the actual events and background of this story but his personal help, advice, and encouragement are greatly appreciated.

I would like to thank Vivian and Derrill Henderson for their invaluable help in every aspect of this work. They gave generously of their time and effort in the preparation, publication, and distribution of this edition.

I also want to thank my Hong Kong comrades for their help and advice and especially acknowledge the assistance of Roger Cyr (who is now deceased), Phil Dodderidge, and Robert Clayton, whose encouragement was a constant source of inspiration.

I want to thank Alan Heisey, who was the first to challenge and encourage me to begin this work, and Dr. Keith Wong, who added his strong encouragement and support.

I also wish to acknowledge the advice and help I received from my agent Arnold Gosewitch.

Introduction

On January 7, 1941, Prime Minister Winston Churchill wrote to
General Hastings Ismay, Chief of Staff of the British armed
forces, the following remarks:

> This is all wrong. If Japan goes to war with us, there is
> not the slightest chance of holding Hong Kong or reliev-
> ing it. It is most unwise to increase the loss we shall suf-
> fer there. Instead of increasing the garrison, it ought to
> be reduced to a symbolic scale. Any trouble arising there
> must be dealt with at the peace conference after the war.
> We must avoid frittering away our resources on unten-
> able positions. Japan will think long before declaring war
> on the British Empire, and whether there are two or six
> battalions at Hong Kong will make no difference to her
> choice. I wish we had fewer troops there, but to move
> any would be noticeable and dangerous.

Later in that year, in complete disregard for Churchill's warning, Canadian troops were sent to defend Hong Kong anyway.

There have been many articles, books, and reports written about the military catastrophe that overtook the British colony of Hong Kong in December of 1941. This narrative has a somewhat different focus from all the other analyses. It is not about the lack of military preparedness, the underestimation of the Japanese, or the lack of air, sea, and land forces necessary for an adequate defence of the island. It is not about the decision of the Canadian Cabinet or its ambitious Chief of the Canadian General Staff, who sent so many needlessly to their death. Indeed, this is the important story that emerges from all the many explanations, justifications, excuses, recriminations, and all the bitter tears about a group of young Canadians whose response, when charged with a hopeless task on a mountainous island 12,000 miles from home, was one of undaunted courage and unswerving loyalty to each other and to their country. It is not about how they failed at Hong Kong, but how they succeeded in that bloody conflict to show the world their mettle. These young men of the Royal Rifles of Canada, under impossible circumstances and against desperate odds, with their backs to the sea, fought to the end without a thought of surrender because of who they were and what they believed in. Despite the odds, they fought until they were ordered to cease fire and to lay down their arms. Today, more than 60 years later, as I think about their sacrifice at Hong Kong, I still marvel at their valour and am proud to say I was one of them.

Chapter One

Enlistment

On September 3, 1939, when Britain declared war on Nazi Germany, I was 17 years, three weeks old. I was living with my aunt and uncle and their two young children in the little town of Listowel, Ontario, approximately one hundred miles northwest of Toronto. I was a Grade 10 student at the Listowel high school, and in those days my enthusiasm for school was limited primarily to the football team.

My mother and father separated when I was 12 years old, and when I was 13 my mother died. After her untimely death, I went to live with my Uncle George and his family. He was a famous, retired professional hockey player and, not only was he one of the greatest players to ever tie on skates, he was one of the finest gentlemen to ever grace the National Hockey League. His picture is prominently displayed today in Canada's Hockey Hall of Fame. Uncle George and his wife, Irma, were wonderful to me and he became my coach in life, my role model, and my best friend. I live by his values and his example to this day.

As Canada had not yet recovered from the crippling Great Depression of the 1930s, my uncle was now forced to look after a needy teenager, as well as his own young family, at a very difficult time for him and for all Canadians. He had lost his considerable fortune in a Florida land deal that went wrong in the Depression, and he was having great difficulty, as a life insurance agent, making ends meet.

My father and mother had met in France in World War I and were married, in Edmonton, after the war. He was a major in the army and she was an army nurse. They both served with distinction and, as their only child, I remember the thrilling stories of their military adventures.

In the winter of 1938, I had joined the local Listowel militia, which was an artillery unit designated the 100th Battery. We were equipped with World War I 18-pound field guns, which were stored in the local armoury. It was as a member of the local militia battery that I began to learn the rudiments of soldiering. I was trained as a signaller and learned to send and receive the Morse code by wireless, flag, and heliograph. As a signaller, I was assigned to the forward observation post, called the "O Pip," with the battery commander, from which by telephone we directed the battery's fire onto its selected targets. From this forward position, I watched the senior officers direct the battery and passed their orders back to the waiting guns. It was a thrilling experience for an impressionable 17-year-old to transmit the orders given and then hear the rounds whistle overhead, on their way to explode on the target.

In the summer of 1939, I went with the battery to Camp Petawawa, where we lived in tents for two weeks of training and manoeuvres. I loved the militia and I was proud of my position as a signaller in the town's prestigious military club. When not in camp, we met after supper every Friday night at the armoury for training in our military specialties and, unknown to my uncle, for a five-cent glass of beer in the gunners' wet canteen. My envious schoolmates disparagingly called us "Friday-night soldiers."

In 1939, Canada, never a warlike nation, had a regular army of only 4,162 men and a non-permanent militia of 51,000 and was in every way woefully unprepared for war. Believe it or not, we had a prime minister who, after a state visit to Germany before the war, widely expressed his admiration for Adolf Hitler — a view, I might add, that thankfully was not shared by many in Canada or anywhere else. I cannot help but imagine Winston Churchill's chagrin when, after spending years trying to warn the Western nations of the dangers of Nazism, he heard of our prime minister's words of praise for Hitler.

Most Canadians were unaware of our unpreparedness for war and we in the militia never dreamed, as we polished our brass buttons, our handsome leather bandoleers, and our spurs, that we were on the brink of a massive military confrontation with Nazi Germany. When, in September of 1939, Germany refused to cease its invasion of Poland, Britain declared war on Germany, and simultaneously Canada's militia, including the 100th Battery, was mobilized from coast to coast in support of the mother country. Within a week, Canada's Parliament had also declared war on Germany.

In the meantime, because I could type, I was assigned to type up the enlistment papers of those members of the battery who volunteered to serve in Canada's wartime forces. My rank was gunner and I was paid the handsome sum of $1.30 per day. I reported to the armoury every morning in my uniform and spent the day typing up enlistment papers and letters for the commanding officer. Talk about an exciting time! No more high school for me — I was employed on more serious business, that of saving my country from the Nazis.

Militia Artillery — Petawawa, 1939.

After a week of trying to reason with me, to no avail, my Uncle George phoned my commanding officer and pointed out that, at 17, I was not old enough to join the army. I was out — and shattered. Since I didn't like school very much and felt that I was a burden on my uncle's family, I was thrilled by the possibility of a glorious military adventure, only to be told that my military career was over after one week! To me, the army meant patriotism, adventure, freedom, and independence. I saw the declaration of war as an answer to my prayers, to be able to strike out on my own in the exciting outside world and, like my parents, serve my country. By now, high school had lost what little interest or appeal it had ever had for me and so, after a week of moping, cursing my birth date, and scheming, I decided to run away from home. I left home one morning at dawn with two dollars in my pocket and hitchhiked to nearby London, Ontario. I left a note for my uncle thanking him for everything and making it clear that I was going to join the army, no matter what!

In London, I went straight to the armoury and, lying about my age, said that I was 18 years old and enlisted as a private in the Army Service Corps. I didn't know what the Army Service Corps did in the army, but I didn't care. I had left home and I was a real soldier now, in a real unit in the army, just as my father and mother had been when they were young. As I look back, there is no doubt in my mind that I was greatly influenced by the military careers of my parents when they had served in Canada's superb army in World War I, and I wanted very much to follow in their glamorous footsteps.

After a few days, I phoned my uncle and told him where I was and what I had done. I said that if he interfered again, I would go out west and enlist again, and sever our relationship forever. My news couldn't have been that bad, because at least he knew where I was and he now had one less dependant to feed and clothe. He had also served in the Canadian Army as a young man, in France in World War I, and he could understand how so many of my age group were attracted to the life of adventure offered by the army.

Being without transportation equipment at this time, the Army Service Corps was trained as an infantry unit, and my training began the next day on the plain behind Wolseley Barracks in London. We lived in tents without floors and slept on palliasses on the ground. There were no indoor toilets or showers. Water to wash and shave came from cold-water spigots hastily installed and attached to wooden washstands in the open. The cooking was done in a tent and we ate on wooden tables in the open at first, later having the luxury of eating our meals in a mess tent. The facilities on Wolseley Plain were primitive in the extreme.

When it rained, since our tents had no floors, our palliasses became sodden islands in the mud, and the edges of our two army-issue blankets trailed in the water, which stood an inch deep on the floor of the tent. Our blankets soaked up the chilled water like a blotter soaks up ink. That year, the fall weather was unseasonably cold and wet and I wonder now that there wasn't a mass desertion simply to escape the misery of that muddy, cold, and miserable camp.

On the contrary, enthusiasm for the army and our daily training was high, and while the complaining reached unheard-of levels, expressed in colourful language, we gritted our teeth and bore it. After two months of this misery, when a contingent of new recruits marched into the camp, we lined their route and with knowing smiles chorused, "You'll be sorry!"

Since I was now six feet four inches tall and had some previous military training in the militia, I stuck out like a sore thumb from the rest of the bewildered recruits. I knew how to salute, polish shoes, wind puttees, and shine brass. I knew my left foot from my right foot and I knew the operations of the Ross rifle as well as the Lee Enfield. This evidence of past training and my enthusiasm for the army, while I was too young to promote, soon got me picked for guard duty at the main armoury in downtown London.

The armoury was also military headquarters for the area. Here I learned, to my delight, that when not on guard duty, sheltered by waterproof sentry boxes, the guard slept in the warm armoury on real beds and ate their meals across the street in a restaurant. The guard were also supplied with brand-new uniforms and equipment, and, because we had to look smart in front of the public passing the armoury, we even had irons and ironing boards and could send our soiled clothes out to the local Chinese laundry. I was learning that while military life was fair, it was fairer for some than it was for others.

After one month of service, we were given 48-hour passes, which meant I could go home to Listowel for the weekend. There, dressed up in my new uniform, I met my envious friends who were still stuck in "Sleepy Hollow" and going to high school.

I liked the army — the discipline, the camaraderie, and above all, the sense of adventure. I lived for the simple pleasures of the day with my comrades and, like soldiers everywhere, gave no thought to tomorrow.

My enthusiasm for military life, however, one day received a major setback. During inspection one day, I was put on report for appearing on the regular morning parade "unshaven." This came as a nasty shock as I thought I was the best turned out soldier on parade and, while I had a little fuzz on my cheeks, I never considered it a beard. For my criminal conduct and this serious breach of regulations, I was paraded before the company commander minus my hat and my belt. As I stood at attention in front of the major of the company, the sergeant-major read out the charge: "Conduct unbecoming." There was a long silence as I felt my confidence evaporate and my heart drop into my boots. Could this be true? What would my uncle say? Finally, the major looked up from the charge sheet and said, "Well, what have you got to say for yourself?" I said, wounded and indignant, "But sir, I *never* shave." There was another long pause and the major replied, "Well, soldier, you will now. Five days confined to barracks."

In the first week of November, we were moved from the muddy plain to the local fairgrounds whose buildings had been converted to comfortable barracks with double-decker steel army beds with real mattresses. Such luxury — central heating, electric lights, hot water, showers, flushing toilets, and a roof over our heads! Slowly, the mob of young recruits began to take the shape of a military unit, as we learned the drill, the special language, the structure, form, and philosophy of the Canadian Army. I declared my aging grandmother, who was having a grim time in the Depression, a dependant of mine and persuaded the paymaster to have her paid a portion of my pay each month, which made her eligible for an additional small dependant's allowance from Ottawa. These added incomes were a great comfort to this wonderful old lady in her last years.

Canada and its people, from coast to coast, were swept up in a patriotic drive to save Great Britain and to defeat the Nazis. Everyone was at work producing war materials and regional differences were forgotten. Partisan politics virtually disappeared and the Canadian people were united in a mighty and righteous cause to support and supply our soldiers, sailors, and airmen, and to win the war. The unemployment and the bread lines of the 1930s began to disappear. Those of us in the service felt this powerful, united, nationwide effort behind us and were proud of our role in this vital struggle against the forces of darkness. We in the services would be the spearhead and the strike force for our righteous cause. We knew as well that we were part of a glorious military tradition established by our fathers and uncles on the battlefields of France in World War I, which had ended only some 20 years before. We knew of our gritty, stubborn stands at Ypres and the Somme and how the Canadians had held the line when others fled the first German gas attack. We knew how the Canadian Corps of only four divisions had stormed and captured the impregnable Germany positions atop Vimy Ridge in four days, after both the British and French armies had lost 100,000 men in failing to take this critical position in four years. We were proud of the fact that, on August 8, 1918, the Canadian corps broke the German line at Amiens and penetrated eight miles in two days, to mark the beginning of the end of German resistance in World War I. Ludendorff, commander of the Germany armies on the western front, called this the German army's "blackest day." We also knew that in World War I, the Canadians, under our brilliant General Sir Arthur Currie, had never failed to take their objective, never lost a gun, never lost a battle, and never retreated in the face of the enemy. Many of our senior officers had fought in that war and had built that reputation. We were all aware and proud of the battle honours listed on our regimental flags, and we knew that many of our current officers had personally fought in those battles in far-off France, when they were young.

It was a Canadian named John McCrae who wrote, "In Flanders Fields the poppies blow, between the crosses row on row." We knew of that sacrifice and of the honour and acclaim they had won, and we were determined that we would live up to the high standards set by our fathers on Flanders Fields in World War I.

It was an exciting time to be free and to be young, to be a soldier, and to be an important part of the Canadian nation girding itself for a decisive showdown with the Nazis. There was a patriotism you could feel that prevailed in the land from coast to coast, the likes of which we have never seen since and probably will never see again.

The members of the Canadian forces were all volunteers. Strange as it may seem today, we believed absolutely in our cause and we knew our age group must serve to preserve our democratic ideas. We never dreamed of the perils ahead and would not concede for a second that we could be defeated. Canada, and its small army, had distinguished itself in World War I and we felt confident that we could live up to, and enhance, the reputation that our fathers had won in that awful war. But what we didn't know was how unprepared we were for the task ahead or what the awful cost would be to remove the threat to Great Britain and defeat the Axis powers in the global conflict that lay ahead.

At this time in our history, Canada was a vast nation geographically but with a very small population of some 12 million, clustered in a narrow band along the American border. As mentioned earlier, we had a small nationwide militia and a very small standing army and an even smaller permanent navy and air force. Canadians of the day perceived no threat to our national security as we had lived in peace for over a hundred years alongside our giant neighbour to the south, with the longest undefended border in the world. Military careers were not much considered in

Canada and not very attractive to our young people, as we were by no means a military nation.

In this relatively new country of Canada, whose people and commerce were still largely devoted to agriculture, mining, fishing, and forestry, with no real military power, there beat a sturdy heart filled with feelings of loyalty for the ruling British monarch and the people and the institutions of Great Britain. This was only natural since, long before confederation, hundreds of thousands of our immigrants had come from England, Scotland, and Ireland. In the early part of the 20th century, even more came from these countries as the railways pushed westward to populate this vast Canadian land. English Canadians especially had strong ties of blood, language, religion, political and commercial institutions, and commerce with the mother country. Given this background of shared values and mutual interests, it is not surprising that so many Canadians felt unquestioning loyalty to Great Britain. Many French Canadians, when they thought about it at all, felt a similar loyalty to our common values and institutions.

In 1939 when Britain was again threatened by her old nemesis, Germany, on our part the question was not *if* we should come to Britain's aid but *how* and *how quickly* could we be of help. It is interesting to note that in the summer of 1939, King George and the Queen conducted a triumphant royal tour across Canada that was met with great outpourings of loyalty and affection by the Canadian people from coast to coast. I know about this tour firsthand because the 100th Battery of which I was a member participated in the great parades and ceremonies of the royal tour and our unit was inspected, in person, by the King and Queen. It was an exhausting tour for the royals if only because of the continual presence of the ubiquitous prime minister of Canada, Mackenzie King, who, undoubtedly to the horror of the royal party, accompanied the visitors from place to place across the entire nation. I have wondered since if that royal tour of Canada in the summer of 1939, just before the war, was motivated entirely by a desire to assure and cement Canada's loyalty to the Crown as the war clouds gathered in Europe and the warning words of Winston Churchill, who saw the Nazi menace for what it was, were heard and heeded in the British Parliament. There was little attention paid in Canada to the pacifists and those who wanted to further appease the Nazi dictator. However, in any event, in the summer of 1939, as Hitler and his gang of thugs completed their plans to attack and conquer Europe, patriotism was widespread and assumed to be a basic prerequisite for Canadian citizenship.

Chapter Two

Wolseley Barracks — Boys' Town

On December 7, 1939, our commanding officer made a very exciting announcement. Our unit had been chosen to be part of the 1st
Division, and the 1st Division was to sail for England in the next
two weeks. This was electrifying news. The unit was heading for
Europe and the war! My excitement was soon dampened and
turned into bitter disappointment as the next day we were told
that only those over 19 and under 50 years of age would be going
overseas with the 1st Division. All of those under 19 years would
be transferred to the training depot of the Royal Canadian
Regiment at Wolseley Barracks, following the unit's departure.

The next two weeks were painful indeed for those of us under
19. We watched from the sidelines with mounting envy as our
comrades departed to their homes for their embarkation leave
and returned to be equipped for their trip to England. Finally the
gut-wrenching day of departure arrived, and as our comrades
marched gaily out through the camp gates with the red shoulder

patches of the 1st Division on their new uniforms and with the band playing "It's a Long Way to Tipperary," we waved them goodbye and good luck.

When they arrived in Europe, the 1st Division wrote a glorious chapter in the history of the Canadian Army. They fought in Sicily, Italy, Holland, and Germany with great distinction as the spearhead of Montgomery's British army. Their war lasted for almost six years of continual fighting and nearly seven thousand of them lost their lives and found a soldier's grave in Europe. What a mighty host they were!

Wolseley Barracks, 1940.

After the sounds of the marching feet and the band music died away, we slunk back to our empty and silent barracks to sit dejectedly on our bunks as the gloom settled on those of us who were left behind. Our military family was gone and as discards and orphans, we knew not what lay in store for us. We soon found out.

The following day, we were transferred to the training depot at Wolseley Barracks, which was now empty as the Royal Canadian Regiment had also left for England as part of the 1st

Division. The regiment left behind their over-age officers and NCOs. These men were veterans of many years of service in the regular force and were the finest instructors in the army. They were to be our mentors. Age and experience were now to teach youth and enthusiasm by precept and example.

Our unit at Wolseley, to the chagrin of its members, was named "Boys' Town." At Boys' Town, the discipline was bound by iron. The rules were "by the book," and now we were under the steely-eyed command not of citizen part-time soldiers, but of regular army veterans. We soon found out there was a vast difference. At our first parade, as they looked at our dress and watched our performance, their eyes rolled upwards to heaven as if pleading with the Almighty to spare them from the sight of such ungainly rabble.

The originality and the quality of the insults and epithets hurled at us in those first few days by our instructors, as we stood rigidly at attention, staring straight head, relieved us quickly of any idea that we were soldiers. They said, among other things, that we reminded them of Napoleon's retreat from Moscow. In their eyes, we were not a unit; we were a shower of idiots and misfits, sent by higher command to try their patience. According to them, even our mothers could not stand the sight of us. It was bad enough to be orphaned from our division, but to be placed under the command of these vocal, choleric martinets added to the trauma of the separation from our units.

Having dashed our illusions, they began to teach us how to be soldiers, from reveille at 6:00 a.m. to parade "dismiss" at 5:30 p.m. There was no time to feel sorry for ourselves. Our instructors believed firmly in the adage, Idle hands soon find the devil's work to do. We were under their constant supervision at all times, and on Sunday they saw to it that we were marched off to church so the local pastors could get in a few well-aimed licks as well. The devil had little opportunity at Boys' Town.

They taught us how to wear our uniforms and how to "bone polish" our boots until they had a mirror finish, including the insteps. They taught us how to shoot and handle the two-inch mortar, the Lee-Enfield rifles, and the Bren gun. They taught us how to use the bayonet, drilled us in unarmed combat, and taught us how to use our respirators in gas-filled chambers. They taught the drill manual until our response to command was automatic. Above all, they taught us that there were two ways to do things — their way or the hard way. We soon learned "their" way was the preferable course to follow. If one soldier messed up, the whole unit was punished by 20 push-ups or 10 laps around the track or one hour of drill with full packs after supper. Talk about peer pressure to do it right and smarten up! We learned that we were not individuals but a unit that must perform as such — weak links were not allowed. You never let the team down.

We also learned that the army was fanatical not only about courtesy and military formality, but also about cleanliness. Every Saturday morning at eight o'clock we were subjected to what was known as "kit inspection" by the commanding officer, the adjutant, and the regimental sergeant-major — the terrible threesome from on high. In this once-a-week inspection, your entire kit — every knife, fork, and spoon, every sock, shirt, mess tin, every piece of web equipment, everything you were ever issued with — was displayed on top of your bed in a precise order, so that any missing article could be identified by its absence at a glance. Every other part of the room had to be scrubbed with soap and water, especially the floor, which under this hygienic assault had gradually become bleached almost white. There was no place for even a speck of dirt in our polished, antiseptic world.

In order to have all metal parts burnished, boots shining, and brass polished, you had to prepare your kit layout the night before, because if you didn't, you would not have sufficient time before inspections in the morning. To solve this problem, we laid out our kit in its polished, pressed, and exact order the night before, and slept on the floor. Early in the morning, we scrubbed the floor, polished the windows, and polished everything else in sight, including ourselves. By 8:00 a.m., each soldier stood at attention by his bed. All was ready for inspection. God help anyone whose kit was missing or not folded, polished, washed, pressed, and burnished to expectations. Not only was he the subject of immediate ridicule, on-the-spot scorn, and embarrassment, he was loudly told he was guilty of the unspeakable and the unpardonable — he had let his comrades down. He would later have ample opportunity to consider his dangerous, criminal behaviour for the next week, as he peeled endless mounds of potatoes after parade. We used to say that to get along in the army, you had to understand one simple rule: If it moves, salute it; if it doesn't move, scrub it with soap and water; and if it still doesn't move, paint it white!

As the days turned into weeks and the weeks turned into months, as our muscles grew and hardened and our skills and co-ordination increased, it was clear to us we were no longer recruits and so we were no longer treated as such. We began to feel we had made the team.

One day stands out in my memory. On this day, we were assembled in the drill hall and permitted to sit on the floor to hear a lecture from a colonel from the office of the Judge Advocate General. He held in his hand a big red book titled *King's Rules and Orders*. He explained that this book, called the *KR&O* for short, contained the legal basis for the armed forces and was the framework for the justice system of the army. He told us that in the future, we would learn much more about *King's Rules and Orders*, but for now he wanted us to understand just one important thing — the army had the power to court-martial a soldier and if it found him guilty of one of two offences, it had the power to execute him by firing squad. The first such offence was disobeying a lawful order from a superior or desertion in the face of the enemy. The second was rape of any female person of any race, colour, or nationality, anywhere and at any time. He then said that the army considered the second offence the more serious and that the army would execute rapists without any sympathy for the perpetrator whatsoever. He said that there was absolutely no excuse for rape and none would be accepted. There was a deathly silence as his message was received by the assembly of male adolescents. So that's how the army felt about crimes against women? We got that message very clearly. I thought my mother would have approved. I am glad to say that no Canadian soldier was ever convicted of either crime, and, in the entire war, only one soldier was executed and that was for murder. I wonder how many cases of rape we would have today if these were the rules and the consequences for violations.

That period of training in Boys' Town, under the watchful eyes of the Royal Canadian Regiment veteran officers and NCO instructors, was a crucial and formative period for the disparate, motley gang of 18-year-old recruits who came from every facet of Canadian life. There were a lot of rules and a lot of regulations. There was a lot of spit and polish and repetitive drill. Reveille sounded at exactly 6:00 a.m. and the bugler blew "lights out" at exactly 10:00 p.m. Morning parade was held at exactly 7:30 a.m. Daily orders were posted at exactly the same place and the same time every day. Infractions of the rules resulted in apprehension and punishment, in exactly the same way, inevitably and invariably. But under the surface of this structured, predictable, routine life there were other more fundamental values being learned. We learned that the antidote to fear and panic consisted of preparedness, obedience, loyalty to your unit and your comrades, and teamwork. These were the bedrock values that made the individual fingers into a powerful fist. These were the values that cemented individuals into a unit. Despite the grim objective of all our training, I can never remember having so much sheer unadulterated fun as I took my place among that irrepressible, unruly gang at Boys' Town in 1940. I entered Wolseley Barracks as a teenaged high-school dropout and emerged a self-confident young man with a clear mission in life — to become a soldier prepared to play a part in Canada's coming struggle.

Chapter Three

The Royal Rifles

By June of 1940, as we were emerging from our recruit training, Canada's war effort had shifted into high gear and tens of thousands of Canadians were entering Canada's army, air force, and navy. New recruits were pouring into hastily built or converted barracks or tent camps, from Halifax to Vancouver, to begin their training. The quartermaster stores at Wolseley Barracks were busy issuing the horde of newcomers with mounds of stuff: boots, overcoats, uniforms, mess kits, blankets, web equipment, kit bags, gas masks, and rifles. The barracks was being expanded and administrative buildings everywhere were being converted into living quarters for the recruits who were arriving every day.

Canadian industry was gearing up and hiring workers to manufacture the seemingly unlimited and urgent requirements of Canada's armed forces. Shipyards were full of the construction of the navy's requirement for boats and ships of every kind. Our factories were tooling up and beginning to produce the heavy equipment and the munitions required for our rapidly expanding armed forces. Planes, guns, tanks, trucks, and every kind of armament were under construction. Ammunition factories were being built and running on three shifts. The garment industry and the manufacturers of footwear were pouring out the military clothing required. Our farmers increased their planting and their output of farm products to meet the growing demand for food, for both domestic and foreign consumption.

The Depression and the unemployment of the awful 1930s was yielding rapidly to the thousands of new orders and contracts issued by the government to civilian suppliers in every industry to meet military demands for everything from airplane propellers to surgical instruments. The unemployment rolls began to fall as fast as the mercury in Winnipeg in January. Workers were needed everywhere. Our miners were working three shifts to keep the output of our smelters and furnaces increasing. The railways were hiring workers, increasing rolling stock, and straining at the seams around the clock to transport this mass of material and humanity to its designated military destinations.

Canadians of all ages, skills, and walks of life were enrolled in this powerful patriotic surge of national will to meet the challenge of the war in Europe. Uncle George, while too old for active service, became an officer in the air force as a flight instructor. Uncle Reginald became a recruiting officer. A Home Guard was formed, made up of World War I veterans, to guard important military installations and infrastructure such as the inter-lake locks and canals from saboteurs. The biggest city, the smallest hamlet, the most modest farm, and every Canadian family felt the quickened pulse, the urgency, and the vibrations as Canada girded herself for the coming struggle against the Axis powers.

When the inevitable shortage of manpower was felt, Canadian women by the hundreds of thousands donned overalls, wrapped their curls in bandannas, entered the factories and picked up the tools of the former workers who were now in the armed forces, met their production schedules, and often did so on three shifts without a murmur of complaint. Our women even learned how to fly four-engined bombers and, to release pilots for combat jobs, ferried them across the ocean to Britain themselves. Every church and social club organized its members not otherwise engaged to knit socks and sweaters for the soldiers overseas. Wolseley Barracks was in tune with this national tide of activity. The square and indeed the neighbourhood resounded to the cadence of marching hard-soled boots and the sergeants' commands. Drafts of soldiers came and went to fill the needs of the expanding army.

One day in the midst of this organized hubbub, I was summoned to the office of the regimental sergeant-major. At Wolseley, this ramrod-straight veteran, with his medal ribbons and his brass-tipped cane, was regarded in rank as only slightly below God. The RSM seldom spoke to mortals like us but when he did, we listened. As I stood at attention in front of his desk, he informed me that tomorrow in Part I orders I would find that I had been promoted to lance corporal. After a pause to let this sink in, he said a few words of encouragement and the interview was over. The next day, the orders were posted and an unmerciful hazing from my friends began. No more fatigues for me. Now I was a non-commissioned officer, the lowest on the totem pole it's true, but nonetheless I was an NCO.

I was assigned to a sergeant instructor as his gopher, assistant, and apprentice. Within another two months or so, I was again appointed, this time to corporal. First I was given a recruit squad to teach them simple foot drill, which is the basis for all recruit training. Then I began to be allowed to teach more interesting subjects such as the use of the Bren light machine gun. I received a big raise in pay; now I was earning $1.75 per day.

Corporal Instructor, Wolseley Barracks, 1940.

By now I was nearly 18, six foot four, and 200 pounds. I had been a quick learner and, despite my age, was learning much of what I needed to know to be an infantry instructor. I soon became a specialist of the Bren gun and could, to the wonderment of my squad, strip it and assemble it blindfolded in seconds. These were happy, if innocent, times. Now I really was a member of the first team, a corporal infantry instructor at 18 — wow! I was on my way.

The summer of 1940 was a blissful period in my young life. I had a car — an ancient Graham Paige I bought for $50. I drove it home for my period of leave and lorded it over my friends who were still in high school. My officers regarded me as a comer. I was just what they wanted: big, strong, quick to learn, conscientious, loyal, and obedient. From my point of view, I was a member of a close-knit family where I was wanted and appreciated and where, in my role, I was a star performer. My mother would have been proud of me. As my length of service and my level of learning increased, so did my self-confidence. I learned that the men under me would ignore my youth if I was prepared to do myself what I expected of them. I also learned that careful preparation, fairness, and interest in the personal life of each soldier were the keys to gaining their co-operation. However, it didn't always work out as smoothly as I wished. One of my bloopers occurred on the crowded main parade square at Wolseley Barracks as the commanding officer approached from the left of my marching squad. I ordered, "Eyes right." Of course, the fiends obeyed me and smartly looked to the right — away from the colonel. It was a long time before I heard the last of that embarrassing mistake.

At the end of September, I was summoned again by the RSM. He informed me that I was to be promoted to sergeant and was to be posted immediately to the Royal Rifles of Canada. He issued me with my orders and my travel warrants and I left the next day. At the same time, two other outstanding young corporal instructors from Wolseley Barracks were sent to the Royal Rifles: "Red" Beatty and Bob Clayton. Bob was nicknamed "Flash" for some of his exploits while on leave and was one of the foundation rocks of the regiment. Both were also promoted to sergeant. Red Beatty was killed in action in Hong Kong and Bob Clayton was severely wounded. Both of these men were wonderful soldiers. Bob Clayton survived his wounds and returned home, where he became a leader and inspiration to his fellow Hong Kong veterans. Bob was in St. Stephen's Hospital during the Japanese attack on the hospital on Christmas Day, 1941, and was forced to watch the horrible atrocities that the Japanese committed in St. Stephen's, including the bayonetting of 70 helpless, bedridden, wounded patients and the rape and murder of the nursing staff.

The Royal Rifles was an infantry regiment with its headquarters in Quebec City. The regiment had been mobilized in July of 1940 and was in need of additional sergeant instructors. The Royal Rifles of Canada was one of the oldest Canadian regiments in existence, having been formed in Quebec in 1862. At inception, the regiment was called the Stadacona Rifles Battalion. In 1877, the name was changed to the 8th Battalion Royal Rifles and, later in

1920, its name was changed again to the Royal Rifles of Canada. Its motto was Volens et Valens (able and willing). The regiment had a long and proud history of service to Canada. It had served in the South African war in 1899 and its battle honours in World War I included Ypres, Festubert, Mount Sorel, the Somme, Arras, Hill 70, and Amiens. These were the great battles of the victorious Canadian Corps, fought on the battlefields of France. The Royal Rifles were in the thick of these battles, and it was here that the regiment earned its extensive battle honours. The men of the regiment were recruited from the Eastern Townships, Quebec, the Gaspé Peninsula, and the Maritimes. Many were farmers, fishermen, lumberjacks, paper makers, and miners. They had long experience as sport hunters and fishermen and had been exposed to firearms from their early childhood. They were used to hard work and life in the open, and they were fit and tough as nails. They were excellent material for the army, and once you were accepted by them and understood their point of view and their sense of humour, they were wonderful to be with. They were generous, full

The corporal and his car.

of fun, gave little thought to tomorrow, and while they made great soldiers, they never lost their rural perspective and never failed to poke fun at the army, its bureaucracy, and its foibles. English was the official language used in the regiment, but many of the officers and men were of French origin and were bilingual.

The officers of the regiment were all from the same area and many of the senior officers were highly experienced veterans who had served in France with the Canadian Corps from 1914 to 1918. Such officers as Home, Price, Young, Bishop, MacAulay and others gave the regiment a fine slate of highly experienced combat veterans of the great Canadian Army of World War I. Regimental Sergeant-Major Leslie Shore, the senior non-commissioned officer, was also a veteran of the British army in World War I. He was an outstanding RSM and kept a watchful, fatherly eye on the likes of Clayton, Beatty, and MacDonell. There was something about Shore that brought out the best in everyone and no one, especially a junior officer, willingly incurred his wrath.

With this group of first-class senior officers and these tough citizen-soldiers, I was proud to be selected to become a member of their team. From now on, I had a new family to belong to and was a step closer to the war.

I proceeded by train to Sussex, New Brunswick, where the Royal Rifles were quartered in new barracks and just beginning their training. I reported to the Commanding Officer, Lieutenant-Colonel Home, MC, who had served as a rifleman in the regiment in World War I in France. He welcomed me and assigned me to D Company, No. 18 Platoon. He told me that D Company had to mount the camp guard on Monday morning and that my first assignment was to prepare the guard for this important ceremony. He pointed out that a fine showing was important to him at this, the regiment's first big, formal ceremony in this camp. By this time it was four o'clock on Friday afternoon. I remember asking, "Sir, do you mean next Monday morning, two days from now?"

He replied, "Yes." I then asked if this company of 120 men had ever formed a guard before, to which he answered, "No." The commander then asked me if I had any more questions, to which I saluted and replied, "No, sir!" I then departed in haste to find Major Parker, who looked upon me as his saviour, sent from on high in the very nick of time to help him prepare for the guard mounting on Monday morning.

Sergeants and warrant officers, 1941.

The training started the next morning at seven o'clock, on the parade square in the rain. By seven o'clock on Sunday night, I had done all I could with my new company. Ready or not, we were going to conduct the guard-mounting ceremony on Monday morning.

As an instructor from Ontario, I made quite a sensation. In the RCR, all drill movements, such as coming to attention, were conducted by raising the right heel 12 inches off the ground and crashing it down precisely beside the left heel. My new company regarded this as the weirdest thing they ever saw. My half-puttees were so even above my double-soled glossy boots, they thought they were painted on. They immediately referred to me amongst themselves as the "quair fella." They said that if I ever misjudged that movement, I'd shear off my left ankle and be charged with committing a self-inflicted wound.

On Monday morning, they did quite well and, I learned, far better than expected, except that the junior officer of the guard tried to inspect their rifle bores without unfixing bayonets, running the risk of getting his throat cut, but that little detail was of small concern amongst the rookies at Camp Sussex. So my life with my new military family began. I had to prove from day one that I knew more about the army than they did. With these tough guys, it was my salvation.

I was given great support and encouragement by RSM Shore. I was given special assignments, such as recruit instructor, and sent to an officers' training centre at Kentville, Nova Scotia, to qualify for a commission. I was now the youngest sergeant in the Canadian Army. I got along well with both my superiors and my subordinates and soon I became an accepted member of that solid, tough, and carefree body from the forest, the farms, the mines, and the paper mills of Quebec and New Brunswick. Just how tough they were was soon going to be put to the test.

The regiment was sent to Newfoundland to guard the Gander airport, the last refuelling stop for Lend-Lease bombers bound for England, and Botwood Harbour, the outlet to the sea for Newfoundland's mineral resources. This guard duty, in the winter of 1940, was cold and boring. While in Newfoundland, the regiment was presented with a purebred Newfoundland dog. He was jet black and looked more like a small pony than a dog. He was named Gander, after the airport. Gander was the biggest dog I had ever seen. He had a heavy, furry coat and webs between his toes and could swim in the cold Atlantic like a walrus. He was soon promoted to sergeant and wore his red stripes on a black leather harness decorated with the regimental badge. He proudly strutted at the head of the band on church parades and fully realized his importance at the head of the regiment. He was very territorial and refused all other canines entry into the barracks. He reasoned he was all the dog the regiment needed. At Shamshuipo, on the day of arrival, some Chinese lured him to the fence, planning to have him for dinner, but Gander escaped after a struggle. After that, Gander lost his faith in the Chinese and would lie in ambush for them when they entered the barracks on business, to the extent that he had to be tied up in the guardroom. He was very intelligent and learned to stand quietly at attention when required. Unfortunately, this magnificent mascot was killed in action, fighting alongside his regimental comrades at Lye Mun Gap on December 19. He was carrying away a Japanese grenade from a group of wounded when it exploded.

Royal Rifles — Sussex, New Brunswick, 1940.

In October 2000, nearly 60 years after the event, Sergeant Gander was awarded the Dickin Medal, sometimes referred to as the "Animal Victoria Cross," for "exceptional bravery and unselfishness" in saving his wounded comrades during the Battle of Hong Kong. This British award was made posthumously at an impressive ceremony at the residence of the British ambassador in Ottawa, by General Sir Rolland Guy of the British Rifle

Corps. No two-legged soldier did his duty any better and none died more heroically than Sergeant Gander.

In the spring of 1941, we were sent to guard coastal defence guns in New Brunswick and we lived part of that summer in tents in the forest along the rugged Atlantic coast. These postings, while perhaps necessary, interfered with the proper training of the regiment, especially in section, company, and regimental manoeuvres and field exercises. But all of this humdrum, routine guard duty came to a sudden end on October 9, 1941.

We were ordered to move to Valcartier Camp, north of Quebec City, at once. When we arrived in Valcartier and entered barracks there, we were told we were going overseas to a foreign posting. Embarkation leaves were granted and new tropical uniforms were issued. The camp was in an uproar as hectic preparations were made for a long journey to some unknown, foreign destination. The excitement was high and we were so glad to be leaving our boring garrison and guard duties behind for our new adventure. Perhaps the tropical kit meant we were bound for the Middle East to serve with the British 8th Army and the war in the desert of East Africa.

After embarkation leaves were over and all necessary kits and equipment were issued, we boarded the train at Quebec City at the beginning of October and, to our surprise, headed west to Vancouver, instead of east to Halifax. At Winnipeg, we were joined by another regiment, the Winnipeg Grenadiers, who would be part of what was to be called C Force. This force of over two thousand men consisted of the Royal Rifles and the Winnipeg Grenadiers and a force headquarters under the command of Brigadier J.K. Lawson.

After four days and nights, we arrived at the docks in Vancouver and boarded the troop transport *Awatea* and a Canadian cruiser, the *Prince Robert*. As soon as the men were aboard our ships, they cast off and headed out to sea, steaming due west into the Pacific.

The next morning, when our sealed orders were opened, we were informed that our destination was to be the British Crown Colony of Hong Kong.

Our first port of call was Honolulu, where we refuelled and took on fresh fruit and vegetables. Our dock was in the centre of Pearl Harbor, and as we saw the American fleet of battleships and lesser vessels lined up side by side at their berths, I remember wondering at their vulnerability to an air attack.

Our next stop was Manila in the Philippines. We were now in the lush green tropics of that latitude and glad of our tropical uniforms. The ships were crowded and the men slept in hammocks below deck. As the weather got warmer, most of them slept on the decks, exposed to the velvet night air of the Pacific and the galaxy of stars overhead.

After 21 days at sea, we arrived at Hong Kong and marched through the colony to our barracks at Shamshuipo in Kowloon on the mainland. The Hong Kong *Telegraph* newspaper came out with its "first-ever" Sunday edition headlined, "Canadian Troops Arrive Here to Reinforce Hong Kong Garrison."

Canadians disembark at Hong Kong, 1941.

Hong Kong was a pleasant surprise. Shamshuipo was a beautiful barracks, with gleaming, one-storey, white concrete buildings surrounded by manicured green spaces and connected by wide boulevards flanked by flower beds.

As a sergeant, I had a private room and a Chinese batman named Ah Sam who looked after my laundry, polished my boots, and pressed my uniforms. Each day, just before dawn at 10 minutes to reveille, he appeared at my bedside with my shaving gear and an oil lamp and expertly shaved me before I arose. This was followed by a steaming cup of hot, sweet tea called "gunfire."

The Sergeants' Mess was a beautiful building, with white-coated Chinese servants and spacious, fan-cooled verandas where drinks were served before dinner.

The city of Victoria, on the island proper, was a beautiful, modern city with a population of over one million citizens.

On the troop ship, I had successfully participated in a non-stop poker game when I was not on duty and when the ship docked, I had five thousand dollars cash in my pocket. When this was exchanged into Hong Kong mex dollars, the currency of the colony, I had 18,000 mex dollars. A Chinese worker at that time earned about 25¢ a day in Hong Kong currency. I was a very wealthy man in a town where a rickshaw ride from the barracks to the ferry docks was 10¢ and a bottle of Johnny Walker Scotch was $1.85. For a 19-year-old who had never been in a big cosmopolitan city in his life, you can imagine what it was like to be in Hong Kong with all that money.

After a cool gin and tonic in the mess, I headed with three or four of my less wealthy friends for the bars, upscale restaurants, and nightclubs of Victoria on the island. Of course I had my own rickshaw boy who met me at the camp gate and stayed with me for the evening until my return to the barracks. If we missed the last ferry boat, we just hired a private motor launch to take us home. The next six weeks were spent exploring the sights, sounds, and delights of this wide-open, bustling, sophisticated Chinese city. I knew why it was called the best possible posting for a British soldier and the "Pearl of the Orient."

Royal Rifles arrive in Hong Kong, 1941.

Within a few days of our arrival in Hong Kong, we were paraded before a solemn-faced British medical officer. We were informed that in Hong Kong any association with the beautiful young Chinese girls we saw in abundance opened up the risk of being infected by a particularly virulent and dangerous form of venereal disease that, according to the doctor, raged unchecked throughout the colony. After his warning speech, the doctor then produced a series of slides projected on a large screen that showed, in graphic detail, the havoc that the disease wreaked on the bodies of soldiers who had had the misfortune to become infected. After these pictures of the symptoms of the disease, pictures were shown of how the disease was treated by the British medical staff. Since at this time penicillin was unknown, I will leave the treatment procedures for this malady to the imagination of the reader, except to say the treatment required hospitalization, was horrific, and was extremely painful. At the end of this presentation, my skin was crawling and I was filled with horror. I knew little or nothing about the fascinating subject of sex, but, to say the least, this did not seem to be a good place to attempt to learn more about it.

After this venereal chamber of horrors was revealed to us, we were then told of the punishment the army meted out to those who contracted venereal disease. This was no joke either. All in all, to most of us these revelations came as a rather nasty shock. It seemed that while Hong Kong had some great attractions, with Chinese girls at the top of the list, there were some serious downsides to fraternization with the locals.

After the medical officer was finished with his doomsday message, we were then addressed by a British warrant officer. He informed us that as Hong Kong was full of thousands of refugee families who had come from mainland China and were literally starving to death, many of these families volunteered a daughter to act as a common-in-law wife/companion to a soldier during his stay in Hong Kong. Once a soldier chose such a girl, he must pay her enough each month to cover her rent, food, and clothing, and that of her family. She, in turn, would act in every way as his common-in-law wife. We were informed that for those who were interested, a Chinese contractor would come to the barracks with a catalogue of pictures of girls who would be willing to enter into such a contract. Once a girl was chosen, she would then be examined by an army doctor, and if she received a clean bill of health, the association could commence. Of course, the British army would deny any involvement in such a scheme, but in their eyes a desperate refugee situation and a need to keep their soldiers from becoming casualties of venereal disease called for unusual measures on the edge of a Chinese mainland torn by the turmoil of war with Japan. We were warned by the British that these girls were often British citizens and that if one entered into a legal marriage with such a girl, under the law she had all the rights of any other female citizen of Britain.

While some availed themselves of this kind of association, such a relationship was not for me. I could not become involved in what I saw as a terrible imposition on the girl. Besides, my mother would never have approved. The partnerships that were thus formed seemed to work very well, and I was told that the loyalty of one of the girls involved extended even to delivering food parcels to her soldier in the Shamshuipo prison camp after he had been captured by the Japanese.

Hong Kong was an exotic port of call full of fascination for its visitors and its soon-to-be defenders from Canada. I was extremely interested in all things military and this interest was heightened when I first saw on the streets of the city the dark-skinned, turbaned members of two famous British-Indian regiments — the Rajputs and the Punjabis. After we had been in Hong Kong about a week, I met a sergeant from the British Middlesex Regiment and invited him to our mess for drinks and dinner. He had served as a regular soldier in the British-Indian army in India for many years before he had been transferred to the Middlesex in Hong Kong and to us he was a fascinating source of information about the regular soldiers of the British Indian Army. He told us that when the British conquered India by defeating its ruling maharajahs one by one in the latter part of the 18th century, they required a large standing army to control and pacify the vast, turbulent, unruly, and sometimes rebellious Indian subcontinent with its many races, languages, and often conflicting religions.

To accomplish this task with a minimum of white British manpower, they recruited into the British army several of the Indian castes or races who had been warriors in India for centuries. These were, to name a few, such races as the Baluchis, Sikhs, Punjabis, Rajputs, Dogras, and, of course, the famous

Royal Rifles march to barracks in Kowloon.

Gurkhas from neighbouring Nepal. Men from these Indian races made superb soldiers and found it easy to serve and swear allegiance to the British Raj. They were recruited often as band boys and apprentices at age 16 and spent their lives as regular soldiers.

When it was time to retire, they returned to their villages with the right to wear their British uniforms and with military pensions for life. Since they had learned many skills in the British army, were relatively well off financially, and were wise in the ways and language of their British rulers, they became an important source of leadership in their villages and demonstrated their loyalty to the British Raj in this role.

The British-Indian army was made up of regiments of one thousand men each. A British-Indian infantry brigade was made up of three regiments. One of these regiments was English, Irish, or Scottish and two regiments were Indian, all of them under the command of a British brigadier and his staff. All the officers in the brigade, down to the level of a lieutenant, were British, and all the non-commissioned officers were Indian. The regimental sergeant-major of a regiment was called a havildar-major and, as the senior NCO, was Indian. The British officers were all graduates of Sandhurst, and only the cream of the Sandhurst military graduation class was allowed to command Indian troops. These officers not only had to be Britain's best but they had to learn and be fluent in the language of their Indian soldiers, whether the troops spoke Urdu or Nepalese.

To us, this was intriguing and showed British ingenuity at its most practical level. To rule India was a gigantic and complex and often dangerous task. To use Indian soldiers who were loyal to the British Crown was one of the British methods to accomplish this task. When we asked about the fighting ability of Indian troops, we were assured they were just as good as any troops in the world and had proved their worth in the past on many battlefields in Europe, the Middle East, and India. The famous 7th Indian Division was at that moment serving in the British 8th Army in the Libyan desert against Rommel's Afrika Korps and was highly regarded for its recent exploits in that theatre of operations.

Canadian contingent in Hong Kong.

A few days later, my Middlesex friend informed us that next Saturday at 7:30 a.m. we would be able to see the 7–11 Rajput regiment on parade for their colonel's inspection. We arrived the following Saturday morning at about 7:20 to see the Rajputs assembled beside the main parade square at Shamshuipo barracks. The Rajputs are a strikingly handsome race. Their skin is a light coffee colour and they have proud aquiline features, with dark eyes and jet black hair. They are tall, the average nearing six feet, and they are beautifully proportioned. As we watched them assemble for parade, we were struck by their quiet, proud bearing and their smiling, happy faces. They were dressed in khaki shorts, puttees, and short-sleeved shirts. They wore striking tan turbans edged with red and black. Their spotless uniforms were pressed to knife edges and their glossy polished boots reflected their impeccable khaki dress.

At precisely 7:30, the havildar-major strutted onto the square and called for company markers. The markers in place, the order "on parade" was given and suddenly one thousand soldiers assembled beside the square began to assemble into sections of 10, platoons of 40, and companies of 120, marching in step towards their appropriate company markers. Without a word of command, as they reached their marker they came to a crashing halt and, again without a command, turned left in unison, dressed to the right, and, when aligned, began to order arms in sequence, commencing with the marker file of three from right to left. These actions were performed in unison, with all the companies on parade acting in concert. Then, as their rifle butts reached the ground, again in sequence from the marker file from right to left, the soldiers stood at ease facing the front.

Now there was total silence and not a single movement as the Rajputs waited for their orders, staring straight ahead, each man in exactly the right place in his section, platoon, and company on the square. The havildar-major issued an order and with a crash of a thousand boots, the regiment came to attention as the officers were called to assume their posts on parade. Then, mounted on a great black charger, the commanding officer appeared, accompanied by his second in command. The colonel and the 2IC dismounted and inspected the troops file by file. After the inspection was complete, the colonel mounted his horse and, standing in his stirrups, addressed his men in their own language for about three minutes.

After the colonel completed his address, they suddenly, without any warning, lifted their rifles and gave three mighty cheers, as if to agree with and confirm whatever their commander had said. I felt my pulse quicken and the hair rise on the back of my neck as I listened to this unexpected response. One could sense immediately that those cheers were from a force totally loyal and totally committed to the will of their commander. You could see the pride these men had in themselves, and their high morale as Rajputs and as professional soldiers of British India.

The colonel then called them to attention and gave the order to fix bayonets. There was a pause to the count of four and then, in exact unison, one thousand polished bayonets flashed from their scabbards to their rifle mounts and glistened like a thousand pinpricks of light in the rosy light of the early morning sun. He then gave the order to march past in columns of platoons while their Rajput brass band struck up a stirring British marching tune. They wheeled into position to obey without a misstep and marched past as the mounted colonel returned their "eyes right" salute, in perfect step and in perfect alignment, with their bayonets glinting and their pendants and regimental flag flying above them in the light breeze.

What a spectacle of martial skill — and what a demonstration of training, parade drill movement, military dress, precision, and military order. I was awestruck at this glittering ceremony and stirred to my soul as column after column of these proud soldiers from India swung by beneath a sea of turbans, arms swinging and bayonets flashing, to the rhythmic thunk-thunk-thunk of their marching feet and the rousing martial music of their band. As a small-town boy from Listowel, it was a sight I never expected to see and one I will never forget. Here was a glimpse of India and her martial spirit beyond my imagination.

Little did I know that no one would ever see such a sight again as this regiment was soon to be destroyed by the Japanese invasion of Hong Kong. And we never dreamed that the mighty British-Indian army, with the end of British influence in India, would soon be disbanded, along with all its fabled warriors and its glittering military pageantry, forever.

The defensive positions on the island for the Rajputs were in cement pillboxes at the waterline, along the coast at Lye Mun Gap. This was where the main Japanese invasion thrust took place, and, and, after a heroic defence in the dark on the night of December 18, in a pall of smoke from a burning oil dump, the Rajputs were finally overrun, outflanked, and virtually annihilated, including almost every one of their British officers. If they had been placed further back on the high ground, above Lye Mun, they could have been more effective against the Japanese invasion but as we will see, this was not the British plan for the defence of the island. Like the Royal Rifles of Canada, the 7–11 Rajputs, despite their loyalty and their courage, were overrun and ceased to exist as an operational unit following the Battle of Hong Kong.

It is interesting to note that it was the 14th British-Indian Army, under General William Slim, who in 1943 fought the Japanese to a bloody standstill at Kohima on the India-Burma border and inflicted on the Japanese the first massive defeat suffered by a major Japanese army in the field. The following year, after the monsoon and after saving India from a Japanese invasion, the 14th British-Indian Army attacked and, step by step, in battle after battle, drove the tenacious Japanese from Burma and, in doing so, inflicted more casualties on the Japanese than all other Allied efforts combined during the entire war in the Pacific. Other battalions of the mighty Rajputs played a major part in this decisive British-Indian army victory and avenged in good measure their fallen comrades at Hong Kong.

Within a few weeks, I had the good fortune to meet a resident of Hong Kong who would show me another facet of this fascinating Crown Colony. He was a Scot who had been educated in Scotland, had served briefly in Scotland Yard in England, and had emigrated to Hong Kong to join the Hong Kong police force. He was in his early 30s, was unmarried, and had risen to become the second-in-command of the famous Hong Kong police drug squad. Hong Kong, from its very inception nearly a hundred years before, had been plagued by the opium trade and its corrupting influence on all it touched. In the early days of the colony, unscrupulous

Englishmen had amassed great fortunes from the opium trade, but the current British administration was trying very hard to stamp it out. My friend was a staff inspector and part of a large anti-drug force made up almost entirely of local Hong Kong Chinese policemen, under the direction of British officers. He told me all about the dangerous Chinese criminal gangs in Hong Kong, called tongs, and how they operated. He took me to his home behind a 20-foot-high wall in Happy Valley where I met his Chinese servants, and he showed me his lifestyle as a senior member of the British government's administration in a very sensitive post. He spoke Chinese, both Cantonese and Mandarin, and when we went out on the town, I was amazed at his fluency and his self-confident ease amongst the Chinese.

One Saturday, he took me shopping in parts of the Chinese quarter of Victoria, on the island where people like us were seldom, if ever, seen. I wanted to buy some presents for my aunt and uncle and my young cousins back home in Canada. His help was invaluable and he was both my interpreter and my bargaining agent with the Chinese merchants. His voluble, pretended outrage in Chinese at the merchants' initial asking price was an act of high drama. He laughed when I said I thought we might be too hard on these poor merchants. He said, "Hell, George, if you don't bargain hard with these people, they'll skin you alive. They love to bargain, it's part of their culture, and make no mistake, they are the best bargainers and the best businessmen in the world."

With his help and my poker winnings, I bought some beautiful objects and silk garments, jade, and exquisitely carved ivory for my family. Unfortunately, they never arrived in Canada as the war intervened, and, no doubt, when the Japanese raided the Hong Kong post office, they wound up in some Japanese officer's possession.

My friendship with the staff inspector was a priceless learning opportunity. My Scottish friend had a strong liking and respect for the Chinese, and because of him I was exposed to a rich and ancient culture and a civilized people whose ancestors were writing sophisticated poetry thousands of years before North America was even heard of. It was through my policeman friend that I developed my appreciation of and my affection for the Chinese. I was beginning to understand that I lived in a big complex world with different races, cultures, religions, attitudes and philosophies that were completely outside my limited knowledge and perspective. Listowel, Ontario, was a long way, in many ways, from here. My time in Hong Kong in 1941 was a wonderful experience at one of the crossroads of the world that enabled me, at age 19, to experience the sheer joy that comes from education and personal discovery.

But, alas, things that are too good to be true never seem to last very long. I was soon to have my lifestyle of a teenage millionaire changed to the absolute opposite end of the scale of human existence, but, like most soldiers, I lived for the day and enjoyed it while I could. The war clouds were gathering. Hong Kong and its British and Indian army garrison and its government leaders seemed blissfully unaware of the growing menace just a few miles north of us at Canton as the Japanese gathered their invasion forces.

Meanwhile, as we were going about our duties and enjoying the amenities of Hong Kong, at Imperial Japanese Army headquarters in Tokyo the newly appointed General Hideki Tojo was putting the finishing touches to the plan for the imminent conquest of greater east Asia, including the British Crown Colony of Hong Kong. The fate of the garrison of Hong Kong had been decided. Churchill's fears were about to be realized. The British Pearl of the Orient was very soon to be attacked simultaneously with the American naval base at Pearl Harbor in Hawaii. These surprise attacks were co-ordinated to the minute to commence on December 7, 1941, and were to signal Japan's invasion, as an ally of Germany, of all of southeast Asia. President Roosevelt was to declare December 7, 1941, a "day of infamy" and it was these Japanese attacks on this day that brought the mighty United States into the war as Britain's ally. Now at last the tide would slowly begin to turn in Britain's favour.

Chapter Four

Hong Kong — The Colony and Its Defences

Hong Kong is located on an island 90 miles south of Canton, just off the Chinese mainland. The island of Hong Kong is 11 miles long and an average of 3 miles wide, consisting of an area of about 29 square miles in total. It was occupied by the British in 1841 and had been ruled by a British governor backed by the British army for a hundred years before we arrived in Hong Kong. It is situated below the Tropic of Cancer and is subtropical. The summer months are hot and humid; the winter months are somewhat cooler. Topographically, Hong Kong island is characterized by steep, granite mountains that rise abruptly from the sea, the highest of which rises 1,800 feet above sea level. There is virtually no flat land anywhere on the island and the city of Victoria is on the northern slope of these mountains. Hong Kong has one two-lane highway that circles the island at sea level.

Hong Kong Harbour, between the cities of Victoria and Kowloon on the mainland, is one of the finest natural harbours in the Orient, and by the 1930s had become one of the busiest of the world, as about one-half of all mainland China's trade funnelled through this port. The population in 1941 was nearly 2 million, mostly Chinese, most of whom were British citizens by birth.

For the defence of Hong Kong, the British garrison had five outmoded, obsolete RAF airplanes, an ancient destroyer, some last-century gunboats, and some wooden-hulled torpedo boats. The island's artillery armament was small in number, ammunition stocks were inadequate for sustained defence, and no modern radio location equipment for accurate counter-battery fire was available. In addition, the island had four under-strength battalions of infantry. The Royal Scots and the Middlesex regiments were accompanied by two regiments from the British-Indian army, the 7–11 Rajputs and the 2–14 Punjabis. To this was added a small force of Hong Kong volunteer militia. Three-inch mortars were available, but they had ammunition for only a little more than five minutes of sustained firing.

In the late fall of 1940, the Chiefs of Staff of the British army, after studying the situation facing Great Britain in Asia, determined that Hong Kong should not be reinforced because "it could not be relieved nor expected to withstand a prolonged siege." At the same time, the governor of Hong Kong, Sir Geoffrey Northcote, requested a complete withdrawal of all British forces from Hong Kong because he believed it could not be successfully defended. In considering the matter of further reinforcements for Hong Kong, Winston Churchill was, as indicated earlier, completely opposed to such an idea.

These were the official views of the governor of Hong Kong, the British Chiefs of Staff, and the prime minister of England, only some nine months before Canada decided to send C Force to Hong Kong.

When C Force embarked at Vancouver for Hong Kong, it sailed without its transport or artillery or armoured vehicles of any kind. It had a few three-inch mortars but little three-inch ammunition. We were promised that this essential armament and transport would follow us by ship at a later date. It never arrived. As we look back on this military catastrophe and we consider the commonsensical views of Prime Minister Churchill, the governor of Hong Kong, and the British Chiefs of Staff with reference to reinforcing a hopeless cause, we can only wonder at the decisions of the Canadian War Cabinet. Why, in the face of this sensible opposition, were they in such a hurry to send a Canadian force to Hong Kong? If they had to send a force to Hong Kong, why send a force that, because of its guard and garrison duties, did not yet have the training to prepare it for combat before it was committed to a theatre of great danger, dominated by a powerful, experienced enemy? These questions have never been answered, but Canadian historians have assured me that we were sent to Hong Kong for purely political reasons to answer the government's critics who claimed that 26 months after declaring war on Germany, Canadian soldiers had not fired a single shot in anger.

When I arrived in Hong Kong and began to appraise the British plan of defence and the resources available to implement them, I began to wonder. First of all, from a tactical viewpoint, there seemed to be no plan to fortify and occupy the high ground in the centre of this mountainous island. The next unsettling fact was that Hong Kong's fresh water, plus 98 percent of its food for a population of over one million, came from the mainland, which supply could easily be cut off by an invader who came by land. There was no airport, military or civilian, on the island. Kai Tak Airport was on the mainland, easily made available to an invader from the land but denied to us.

The local British commander, Major-General Maltby, seemed to believe that the present British garrison would be adequate to defend the extensive coastline while his superiors in London felt that an adequate defence would require at least another full division. The British believed the Japanese soldier was inferior. We heard from them that the Japanese had very poor eyesight and that they couldn't shoot infantry weapons accurately and that their pilots, due to the same optical weakness, couldn't put their bombs on target. Above all, not to worry, the Japanese couldn't fight at night. Of all the mistakes Maltby made, his unquestioned basic assumption of the Japanese lack of military skill and general incompetence was one of the most serious. Once top commanders are guilty of underestimating their enemy, trouble for the soldiers below is not long in coming. As we were soon to find out, the Japanese army was specially trained to attack and fight at night.

Before long, I could see that if the Japanese attacked, since our naval forces had been withdrawn to Singapore, we could not be supplied, we could not be reinforced, and we could not be evacuated. This was not Dunkirk on the English Channel, a few miles from England. Hong Kong was an isolated, unprepared military death trap. If the Japanese attacked, we had two options: we could die on the battlefield or become prisoners of a savage enemy who was not even a signatory to the Geneva Convention on the treatment of prisoners of war. I can just imagine the feelings of our veteran senior officers after they unpacked and began to assess the military situation they now faced. If I, at my level, could see the defence problems even dimly, imagine what they saw through their experienced eyes. I can only guess that our senior officers hoped the Japanese would not attack Hong Kong and that we would be transferred to the European theatre of war when it was appropriate to do so.

I suspect my company commander, Major Parker, shared my anxiety about our vulnerability from the high ground because, after we had been in Hong Kong for a week or so, he sent for me. He gave me a large map of the island and instructed me to take some of my men and climb up to the high ground above Ty Tam Tuk Reservoir and explore and mark on the map the route that could be followed from Mount Butler west to the highway below Aberdeen.

We assembled and, equipped with compasses, binoculars, and instructions, climbed up to the elevation required and surveyed and marked the route we could follow to Aberdeen and the highway to the west. We were careful to mark all water catchments, barbed wire, and any pillboxes or defensive works we came across. At the end of the reconnaissance, I went over our findings with Major Parker in detail. The answer to his question concerning anything that would deter an enemy from moving across the same route from Mount Butler was summed up by me as "practically nothing." We never saw a single British soldier or any serious, man-made impediment to an invading force moving west from Mount Butler to Aberdeen. Within a few weeks, that is exactly what the 229th Japanese Regiment did to split the island defending forces in two and find and kill Brigadier Lawson, our Canadian brigade commander, at his HQ at Wong Nei Chong Gap.

Major Parker had reconnoitred the high ground from Mount Butler east to Sai Wan, and together we joined the two routes in a meeting at company HQ included our platoon commanders and our second in command. While Parker never expressed his thoughts in my presence as he listened to my report, I could sense his deep concern about the information. As I understand it, General Maltby, the British officer commanding the forces at Hong Kong, simply did not share our concern with respect to the undefended nature of the island's high ground. This failure to consider the importance of the high ground became one of the first issues of tension and serious disagreement between the British and Canadian high commands at Hong Kong. Of course, even if Maltby had been persuaded of the merits of the Canadian argument, it was too late to do anything about it anyway. At the same time as our senior officers at Hong Kong assessed the threat to their command, they were severely handicapped both at Hong Kong and at army headquarters in Ottawa because of their lack of factual, substantive intelligence. Lack of appreciation for the size, power, and effectiveness of the battle-tested Japanese armed forces, who had been fighting in China since 1937, coupled with an assumption of their poor quality, was to lead to a military disaster and the elimination of the Allied forces at Hong Kong.

Chapter Five

The Battle for Hong Kong

At 8:00 a.m. on December 8, 1941, the Japanese struck. This attack was timed to coincide with the bombing of the American naval base at Pearl Harbor. Waves of Japanese bombers attacked the colony without warning and in a matter of minutes had destroyed our air force on the ground at Kai Tak Airport. Simultaneously, the Japanese army attacked the outer perimeter of the land-based defences in the New Territories on the mainland. This heavy and skilfully led attack forced the British, Indian, and Canadian defenders to gradually retreat, and by December 13 at 9:20 a.m., all forces in the New Territories were withdrawn to the island. It had taken the Japanese only five days to gain absolute control of the mainland. The British commander, General Maltby, estimated the Japanese invaders to number 60,000 men, with modern artillery and tanks.

On December 8, James L. Ralston, Minister of National Defence, cabled Brigadier Lawson from Ottawa: "Concurrently with the Dominion's declaration of war against Japan, I send you the assurance of complete confidence that the forces under your command will, in the days that lie ahead, worthily uphold the best traditions of Canadian Arms."

On the 13th of December, a document signed by General Sakai and sent across the harbour under a flag of truce requested the defenders to surrender to save further bloodshed. The request was refused categorically by the British governor, Sir Mark Young. Now the enemy began to shell, bomb, and mortar our coastal defence works and began to pound our concrete pillboxes to rubble. The Lye Mun defence area was especially subjected to a fierce and continual bombardment.

At 9:30 a.m. on December 17, the Japanese commander, General Sakai, sent another white flag of truce across the water, accompanied by another request to surrender. Again, the Japanese offer was rejected. The Japanese, when they considered our positions and our options, expressed surprise at our rejection of their offer.

On the 18th of December, at 10:30 p.m., the Japanese began to land in great force at four different locations on the northeast side of the island, under a dense smoke screen caused by the fires from their heavy shelling and bombing of the area. The Japanese poured ashore and in a few hours during the night of December 18–19, overran the Rajput

Brigadier J.K. Lawson, Canadian commander at Hong Kong.

defenders in fierce fighting, killing most of their officers and virtually wiping out the regiment. Next, they overran the Canadian defenders at Lye Mun, inflicting heavy casualties, and by sheer weight of numbers they infiltrated and penetrated our prepared lines of defence. Japanese intelligence was excellent and found on dead Japanese officers were multiple copies of British military maps of the island and its defence positions.

Lawson now received a second cable, this one from Prime Minister Mackenzie King: "All Canada has been following hour by hour the progress of events in Hong Kong. Our thoughts are of each and every one of you in your brave resistance to the forces that are seeking to destroy the world's freedom. Your bravery is an inspiration to us all. Our country's name and its honour have never been more splendidly upheld."

After their first lodgement, Japanese reinforcements came ashore in successive waves and began to rapidly ascend the high ground, killing and driving back any defenders who stood in their way. During this thrust to secure the high ground in the centre of the island, the Japanese broke through to Brigadier Lawson's brigade headquarters at Wong Nei Chong Gap and killed the brigadier and his entire staff, except for a captain who was badly wounded and left for dead.

Now Canadian communications were severed and the island's defenders cut in two by powerful Japanese forces who occupied the high ground and began to increase their advantage by well-armed reinforcements. This violent thrust of the Japanese, under cover of night, forced a contraction of the Canadian lines to a wide semicircle in front of the Stanley Peninsula, and made the peaks overlooking the peninsula the battleground for the opposing forces. Commencing on the morning of the 20th of December, again and again, the Royal Rifles attempted in broad daylight, without any supporting mortar or artillery fire, to counterattack the Japanese positions on

Canadian Bren gun team.

top of prominent peaks such as Sugar Loaf Hill, Boa Vista, Notting Hill, Bridge Hill, Red Hill, Brick Hill, Violet Hill, and Stanley Mound. This entailed scaling the heights with their thick cover of entangling scrub in the face of grenades, enemy machine guns, and mortar fire from above. In each case, by the time we finally reached the top of these peaks and drove the Japanese off, we were out of water, had no food and little ammunition, and were nearly dead from the exhaustion of the day's climb and battle in the heat. Colonel Stacey, in his *Official History of the Canadian Army in the Second World War*, states that in no other theatre of operations did Canadians face such steep and rugged terrain or suffer so much from such difficult ground. The physical effort to climb these tangled, scrub-covered slopes, loaded down with weapons, water, and ammunition, was a major effort in itself. To do it all day and almost every day in the face of a determined, well-led enemy, who had to be killed to be evicted, led to mind-numbing exhaustion. In these conditions, to keep men and units together in some form of order and evacuate the wounded was a nightmare. The undergrowth was so thick and the slopes so steep that many of the dead and wounded were never found and lay where they fell, at the bottom of some tangled ravine or scrub-covered fissure.

As soon as it grew dark, fresh Japanese troops would mount an attack to regain any ground we had taken from them during the day. Under pressure from these attacks and now with no food, water, or grenades, and with little ammunition, we were forced down the mountain with the wounded we could carry, to find ourselves at midnight back at our starting point.

When dawn broke, as soon as water and food (bully beef and biscuits) and ammunition were brought up, the men were awakened and we would be ordered to do the same thing again, each time within a smaller perimeter and with fewer men. The utter futility and agony of these attacks have haunted my dreams to this day. The Japanese outnumbered us by a substantial margin. They were well-led, veteran troops. When we stopped them in some position, they would immediately and skilfully begin to slip around us to turn our flanks, until, to avoid encirclement, we were forced to give ground and reduce our perimeter yet again. They were equipped with mobile mountain batteries and mortars, which were transported by mules. Their mountain battery equipment and mule transport gave them an enormous advantage. They were superb at camouflage and field craft and their organization and fire discipline were excellent.

Now it became apparent that the propaganda to the effect that the Japanese were inferior troops was utterly false. Brigadier John Masters of the British army fought for months against the Japanese in the Burma Campaign and had this to say about the Japanese as an enemy:

They are the bravest people I have ever met. In our armies, any of them, nearly every Japanese would have a Congressional Medal of Honour or a Victoria Cross. It is the fashion to dismiss their courage as fanaticism but this only begs the question. They believed in something and they were willing to die for it .... what else is bravery? They pressed home their attacks when no other troops would have done so.... The Japanese simply came on using all their skill and rage until they were stopped by death. In defense, they held their ground with a furious tenacity that never faltered. They had to be killed company by company, squad by squad, man by man, to the last.

I am glad to say that, faced with such a formidable, better equipped, and more experienced enemy, I never saw or heard of a single soldier in my company who failed to carry out his orders, whatever they were, to hold or to attack. The men of D Company faced the enemy and fought without respite as an organized, coherent unit until it was ordered to cease fire and lay down its arms at 8:30 p.m. on Christmas Day.

I have selected two actions — one on the 20th of December and the other on the 25th of December, the last day of resistance — to describe in more detail counterattacks that took place on my narrow front and through my eyes. I have chosen these two actions because descriptions of them were recorded soon after the armistice, at the request of our company commander, Major Parker.

On the 20th of December, D Company was ordered to attack the Japanese in the centre of our defensive perimeter towards Violet Hill and Wong Nei Chong Gap and, on the way, to find and silence a Japanese battery that had been established somewhere at Tai Tam Tuk Reservoir. Because I had personally recon-

The Hong Kong battlefield — December 18–25, 1941.

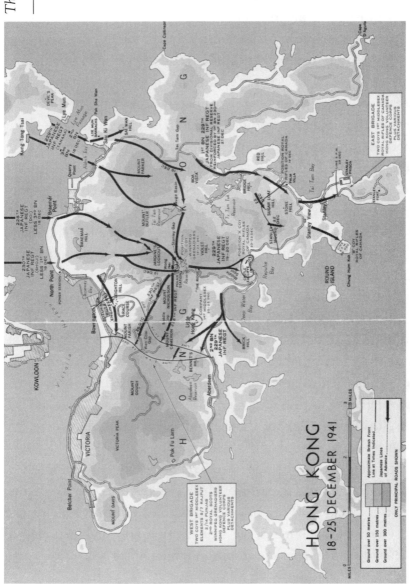

noitred the water catchments in the area earlier in the month, before the Battle of Hong Kong had begun, I volunteered to lead my platoon in this attack. I believed we could penetrate the Japanese line by using the now dry beds of the water-catchment canals to conceal our advance until we could at least get very close to the enemy battery at Tai Tam Tuk Reservoir, which was between us and Violet Hill.

We carried as much ammunition as we could and began our stealthy approach towards the unsuspecting enemy, using the bottom of the water catchment canals as cover. The approach march, or rather crawl, was nerve-wracking, and the risk of discovery rose with every yard we covered. Fortunately, from time to time, the noise of the battery firing masked any noise we made. By about 12:30 a.m., my men were undetected and in position in a water catchment about five feet deep and four feet wide, slightly above and across from the location of the battery. The enemy was within two hundred yards. We had a clear field of fire, with the sun over our right shoulders. Just as I was about to give the command to fire to my waiting gunners, a Japanese staff car drove up with a high-ranking Japanese officer. The car stopped to let its passengers debark, right under the muzzles of our guns. Talk about being in the wrong place at the wrong time! Just as the Japanese officer and his aides stepped out of his car, our weapons opened fire. The chaos was indescribable. The staccato roar of the machine guns, the screams of the unfortunate pack mules, the cries of the surprised Japanese as they struggled to locate their attackers, and the ear-splitting eruptions of their exploding ammunition filled the air with the awful sounds of the carnage.

In a few minutes it was over. The devastation was complete, as fires crackled and wreaths of black smoke curled up to the sky, over the wreckage of the now silent battery. By this time, we had consumed all but our reserve ammunition and had also alerted other supporting Japanese troops in large numbers on Violet Hill

Ty Tam Tuk Reservoir.

above our catchment, which, for its purpose, snaked along the valley bottom. We now had to exit quickly because the sunken water catchment was an untenable place to be with an alert and outraged enemy in force above us on the high ground. I ordered my men to retire as fast as they could run with their equipment, down a water catchment that would lead us back to a position near our starting point, while I brought up the rear to slow down, with my Bren gun, the expected pursuit.

We went down the catchment in the valley to escape, and the Japanese ran along the ridge lines above us to cut us off. Any attempt to proceed on to Violet Hill now was seen to be impossible. The enemy was there ahead of us in force. We were heading for a place where the tree cover made it possible to leave the water catchment and, at the same time, where flatter and more heavily wooded terrain would enable us to better our position. But now our luck appeared to have run out. When I arrived at our exit point from the water catchment, with the sound of pursuit in my ears, I found my men pinned down to the bottom of the concrete catchment by a Japanese Nambu machine gun raking the flat, open ground of our only escape route. While this enemy gun, 175 yards away, commanded our exit from its vantage point above us, we could not leave the protection of the water catchment without being massacred in the open. At this point, another Japanese gun began to enfilade the catchment so that we could not stay where we were either, without being riddled from this second menace. As the seconds ticked away, the catchment escape route became a killing ground for our pursuers. We were in deadly peril. I also knew that only minutes behind, we were being pursued by another enemy force that was following along the same catchment. For sheer, heart-stopping terror, it had no parallel. We were trapped!

As I crashed to the bottom of the catchment to avoid a burst from the gun across the open space above us, one of my corporals said, "Sergeant, what will we do now?" I had no intention of surrendering. My only thoughts were about how I was going to get my men out of this trap. I shouted to the corporal, "Get two Brens and load them with tracer mags, and get them here quick, man!" I then raised my head and put my binoculars to my eyes to locate the Japanese gun across from us. As I lowered my glasses, the first loaded Bren was shoved into my hands. Within another second or so, I had flattened the gun's bipod and laid it flat on the parapet of the catchment, with sights set at two hundred yards.

My enemy across the open ground saw my attempt to mount my gun and we both opened fire at each other at almost the same instant. Because I was firing tracer bullets, I could see my fire plunging into the exact spot where I had seen the earlier movement. As I pressed the trigger in long bursts, I heard his incoming bullets "chirp" as they passed my left ear by less than a 16th of an inch. I roared to my men, "Get ready to cross the open space when I give the order." At the same moment, I focused on where I thought the second, slightly more distant gun was located and began to hose its suspected locality with tracer. I fired burst after burst, non-stop. In the middle of the fourth or fifth magazine, I roared to my men to go. Never did a group of men leave a water catchment and cross 75 yards of ground so speedily! When neither the first nor second Japanese gun tried to intercept this move to escape, I clambered out of the catchment myself and joined my men as we ran for the cover of the trees.

To this day, we don't know what happened to the Japanese machine gunners who had us trapped in the catchment. At any rate, they stopped firing and we escaped. How we managed to get so close to the battery without detection was probably due to the Japanese ignorance of the existence of this particular water-catchment labyrinth — and the audacity of such an attack in broad daylight. After our surrender, the Japanese tried to find out from us who had led the raid on the battery, but a wall of Canadian silence finally discouraged their investigation. The miracle of it all was that not one of my platoon was killed that day, and only six were wounded.

At dawn on the 25th of December, the exhausted survivors of the Royal Rifles, finally pushed out of the hills, had retreated to Stanley Fort at the end of the Stanley Peninsula. It was here that we planned to make our last stand. I had buttoned into my shirt pocket one last bullet for myself. I had no intention of being taken alive after seeing how the Japanese tied their prisoners' hands behind their backs and used them for live bayonet practice. I intended to avoid such a grisly end.

At eight o'clock on Christmas morning, I was called to an officers' conference. Here we were told that my company, D Company, was ordered to sally forth from the fortress and attack Stanley Village, a quarter of a mile below us and occupied by the Japanese. Our mission was to retake the village that had been lost the day before and drive the Japanese from it. The counterattack was to commence at 1:00 p.m.

The sheer stupidity of the order to send us without artillery, mortar, or machine gun support into a village full of Japanese, in broad daylight, was not lost on me. I was given the task of attacking the left flank of the village and securing a row of houses, which would give us an excellent field of fire across the village. As I heard these orders, my heart sank. My men would be attacking in the open and the Japanese defenders would have excellent cover from which to repel us. This was madness! As I walked back to prepare my men for the coming assault, I realized that this would be my last day on Earth. I could see that finally my luck had run out. When I returned to my platoon, I told them of our orders to mount an attack of company strength to clear out Stanley Village at 13:00 hours. There was complete silence as they stared at me through their exhausted and unbelieving eyes. What a preposterous order to men who were so fatigued they could hardly stand! I said something to the effect that attacking the village was no worse than sitting here waiting for the inevitable last attack. Not a single soldier asked to be excused. Those who could stand took part in the attack without a single exception. Since two of my corporal section leaders had been killed in the last two days, I appointed two new section leaders and organized my remaining men into their attack formations. We cleaned our weapons, replenished our ammunition and stock of grenades, and then lay down again to sleep until it was time to form up for the attack.

We assembled at our start line on time and I led my men, crouched low in the ditch beside the road, into the village from the main entrance of the fort. The enemy opened up with machine guns, mortars, and small-calibre artillery. By crouching low and dodging from rock to rock, we managed to reach a piece of dead ground one hundred yards from the outer perimeter of the village, with no casualties. In front and slightly above us was a graveyard that lay to the west of our objective. I ordered my men to spread out in a skirmish line, facing the graveyard. Since the enemy had taken up a much superior position above us in the graveyard and we were in the open, I decided we must close quickly or suffer heavy casualties. As soon as my men were spread out on either side of me, I ordered them to fix bayonets and charge. Within seconds, emitting fearful war whoops, we were upon the enemy in the graveyard, firing our shoulder-slung Bren guns from the hip. This manoeuvre took the enemy by surprise. A confused and bloody melee of hand-to-hand fighting with bayonets then took place.

In no more than one or two minutes, we had overrun the Japanese and cleared the graveyard. We then carried on and pursued the fleeing Japanese survivors to the first line of houses, where they took a stand to repel us. Another hand-to-hand battle erupted as the Japanese stubbornly refused to be evicted. We tossed in grenades and cleared the houses with our tommy guns and bayonets. We passed through these first houses and entered a north-to-south street in the village. There, as we turned a corner, we ran into a platoon of unsuspecting Japanese riflemen running forward with their rifles at the trail, presumably to reinforce the unit we had just overcome. As we were spread out and prepared for anything, we opened up with a roar of machine-gun fire and literally wiped out the oncoming force, which had been taken completely by surprise at our presence.

We carried on and finally reached and passed the line of houses, which was our objective. A British officer who witnessed our attack wrote, "We saw the last glorious charge of the Canadians, up through the graveyard and into the windows of the bungalows at the top. We saw the Japanese escaping through the back of the houses and their return with grenades, which they lobbed amongst the Canadians in occupation. Very few Canadians survived that gallant charge." We were now well into the village, and our fire was creating havoc among the Japanese. Now the enemy began to stiffen their resistance and we began to take casualties from their return fire. I ordered the men back to our assigned objective and we took up positions in and around the houses and began to pour a heavy fire on the counterattacking Japanese. At this point, a runner from No. 17 platoon on our left told me that Lieutenant Power had been killed and, therefore, I assumed command of No. 17 platoon as well. Sergeant Lance Ross from No. 17 Platoon joined me and with our Lewis and Bren guns we repulsed the Japanese with a murderous fire.

There was now a lull as the Japanese regrouped, brought forward reinforcements, and registered their artillery on our position. This pause gave me a chance to assess our position. We had taken many casualties and were running out of ammunition. One of the section leaders, Corporal McLellan, was killed and another severely wounded. We were out of water, it was hot, and we were suffering the pangs of thirst. After about 20 minutes, the Japanese remounted their attack and, as usual, began to outflank our position. At the same time, their artillery began to fire shells into our positions in the houses. With the houses literally being shot to pieces around us, the enemy outflanking us, casualties rising, and my ammunition running low, I was relieved to receive an order carried by a runner to pull back, as I was about to be encircled and cut off.

I sent the men back in small parties, while Sergeant Ross and I covered them with our machine guns and the remaining stock of ammunition. My wounded, who could not walk, lay where they had fallen. I left first while Sergeant Ross covered me, and then he ran back as I covered him. Finally, by some miracle, we both made it to a drainage ditch that allowed us to crawl out of range. It was impossible to evacuate our wounded; the Japanese were now so close and so positioned that to retrieve them would have been suicidal. I would certainly have lost all of both platoons in the attempt. And so these brave young men were left where they lay, at the mercy of their enemy. As we retreated back to the fortress, we met Major Parker. He told us we were the last to leave the village. It was now after 6:00 a.m. and the three of us finally entered the fortress just as the sun was setting.

That day, D Company lost 84 percent of its original force of 120 men in Stanley. Twenty-six men were killed and 75 were wounded. I recommended Sergeant Ross for the Military Medal for his courage and his coolness under fire. That night, as we prepared for the next and last Japanese onslaught, we were informed at 8:30 that the governor, Sir Mark Young, had surrendered. We were ordered to cease fire and lay down our arms. It was over!

The next day, I took a group of unarmed men back to the battle area in the village to find and bury our dead. The Japanese were doing the same and were laying out large numbers of their dead, side by side, to be cremated. We found our men where they had fallen and in the village we dug and marked a shallow grave for each. As we sadly consigned them to their soldiers' graves, we bared our heads, and I said a few simple words over each and bade them farewell.

Military historian Carl Vincent, in his definitive book, *No Reason Why*, on the Battle of Hong Kong, writes that D Company's Christmas Day attack on Stanley Village "for idiotic futility ranks with the charge of the Light Brigade." Today, more than 60 years later, as I recall these actions, I am both proud that I was a member of that courageous band and full of sorrow. To this day I am haunted by the tragic and unnecessary loss of those young lives. Given what had transpired in the week before and the men's state of exhaustion, I still marvel at their courage and their willingness to die rather than fail to do their duty.

Back in Ottawa, in the middle of Christmas celebrations, in the rhetoric of the day after the news that Governor Young had surrendered the island to the Japanese, Defence Minister Ralston declared, "Reports make it abundantly clear that the Canadians shared in fullest measure, in the steadfastness, the endurance and the heroism of this epic battle." Thus the Royal Rifles and the Winnipeg Rifles of C Force at Hong Kong were the first Canadians to engage the enemy in World War II. Those who survived the battle and imprisonment were also the last to wend their weary ways back to their homes after the war.

The treatment of those of our men who were unlucky enough to be wounded or taken prisoner by the advancing Japanese at Hong Kong can only be described as barbaric. During the battle when we had recaptured a position, we often found the dead and mutilated bodies of our men who had been made prisoners or had been wounded. During the trials for war crimes that followed Japan's surrender, Japanese behaviour both during the fighting on the battlefields and after the war in Hong Kong's prison camps was made public. Among the 53 Japanese indicted for war crimes at Hong Kong were four senior Japanese officers: General Sakai and Colonels Shoigi, Tokunaga, and Tanaka. They were charged with the responsibility during the fighting for the execution of many unarmed and wounded prisoners, many with their hands tied behind their backs and some in hospital beds, by bayonetting, shooting, or beheading by sword.[*] Captain M. Banfill, a doctor in the Canadian Medical Corps, testified at the Tanaka trial that after his medical outpost had been overwhelmed at the Salesian Mission on the 19th of December, the Japanese murdered in cold blood 15 Canadian and British soldiers and 21 civilians, including nine nurses and two doctors, by lining them up to face a precipice and then bayonetting them in the back. A second witness and victim himself to this massacre was Corporal

---

[*] Lieutenant General Sakai and his 38th Japanese Infantry Division, with major support from other units of the 23 Japanese Army, were the enemy troops who captured Hong Kong. This veteran division, after making up its casualties suffered at Hong Kong, soon sailed for the South Pacific where it fought with great distinction. It was here, within a year, that the tide of conquest turned against Japan and the 38th Division met its fate. In the steaming jungles of Guadalcanal and New Guinea, the 38th Japanese Infantry Division was completely annihilated at the hands of the U.S. Marines and the Australians. General Sakai was executed in 1946 for, among other things, the murders at St. Stephen's Hospital in Hong Kong on Christmas Day 1941.

N.J. Heath of the Royal Army Medical Corps. He received a sword cut from behind at the base of his skull and collapsed. He survived only because he was left for dead, covered by his dead comrades in a pool of blood at the foot of the cliff.

At Eucliffe House on Repulse Bay, Lieutenant C.D. Johnson of the Royal Rifles testified that as a member of a burial party, all the Canadian bodies he found there had been beheaded, with their hands tied behind their backs. Lieutenant-Colonel John Crawford of the Canadian Army Medical Corps testified that at one site he found 12 bodies and at another, 20 bodies. He stated at the trial that, "I formed the opinion that all of these bodies had been bayonetted. They could only have arrived at the spot where they lay by having fallen or having been thrown from the parapet above."

Testifying at Prime Minister Tojo's trial before the International Military Tribunal for the Far East, Captain James Barnett, padre for the Royal Rifles, described how on Christmas Day, December 25, the Japanese broke into St. Stephen's Military Hospital and bayonetted to death as they lay in bed 70 helpless wounded soldiers and raped, murdered, and dismembered nurses. There were no arms or armed soldiers in the hospital and there was no known provocation for this horrific attack on a hospital full of wounded, prominently displaying the Red Cross symbol. He himself was saved only because the governor surrendered the island during the day. He was then forced to cremate, without creating any records of the dead, 170 bodies.

In 1948, the International Tribunal for the Far East reported that:

> The evidence relating to atrocities and other conventional war crimes presented before the Tribunal establishes that from the opening of the war in China until the surrender of Japan in 1945 torture, murder and rape and other cruelties of the most

inhumane and barbarous character were freely practised by the Japanese army and navy. During a period of several months, the Tribunal heard evidence, orally or by affidavit, from witnesses who testified in detail to atrocities committed in all theatres of war on a scale so vast, yet following so common a pattern in all theatres, that only one conclusion is possible — the atrocities were either secretly ordered or wilfully permitted by the Japanese Government or individual members thereof and by the leaders of the armed forces ...

From beginning to end, the customary and conventional rules of war designed to prevent inhumanity were flagrantly disregarded. Ruthless killing of prisoners by shooting, decapitation, drowning and other methods; death marches in which prisoners including the sick were forced to march long distances under conditions which not even well-conditioned troops could stand, many of those dropping out or bayoneted by guards; forced labour in tropical heat without protection from the sun; complete lack of housing and medical supplies in many cases, resulting in thousands of deaths from disease; beatings and torture of all kinds to extract information as confessions or for minor offenses; killing without trial of recaptured prisoners after escape and for attempting to escape; killing without trial of captured aviators; and even cannibalism: these are some of the atrocities of which proof was made before the Tribunal.

After the war, military tribunals found guilty and executed 920 Japanese for war crimes that included even acts of cannibalism on Allied soldiers. Many of them were Japanese officers and three of them, Tojo, Yamashita and Homma, were well-known, high-ranking Japanese generals. Colonel Isao Tokunaga, the senior officer in command of all prisoners of war at Hong Kong, after his trial for war crimes against Canadian and British internees at Hong Kong, was sentenced to death for, among other things, the murder of four Canadian and five British prisoners of war. This sentence was commuted to "life" and then to 21 years.

In all, 53 Japanese were indicted for war crimes ranging from outright murder to death caused by prolonged torture of both civilian and military personnel under their control at Hong Kong from 1942 to 1945. It has been established by the International Tribunal that 4 percent of Allied prisoners held by the Germans and Italians died, while 27 percent of all prisoners captured by the Japanese died in captivity.

The civilized world found it almost impossible to believe that Japan's military leaders were capable of, and indeed wallowed in, such studied, callous brutality and mind-numbing atrocities as were revealed in their indictments for war crimes after the war. I can understand why, for purely practical reasons, the United States avoided trying Emperor Hirohito as a war criminal, but I still find it difficult to understand why he himself did not curb his officers and prevent them from behaving like savages across his conquered territories. As the International Tribunal stated in its report, "the atrocities committed ... on a scale so vast yet following so common a pattern ... that only one conclusion is possible — the atrocities were either secretly ordered or wilfully permitted by the Japanese Government or individual members thereof and by the leaders of the (Japanese) armed forces."

The loss of Hong Kong in 1941 was a humiliating defeat for the British at the hands of the Japanese. It was the beginning of the end of the British Empire. Years of military neglect, glaring underestimation of the Japanese, unpreparedness, poor leadership, and wishful thinking finally led to disaster. That the British would allow their Canadian allies to send reinforcements to Hong Kong, knowing what they knew about the strategic situation and the island's defences, is reprehensible.

For the Canadian families who lost a father, son, brother, uncle, or cousin, it was a needless tragedy. It altered for the worse even the lives of those who survived and, as I can personally attest, placed heavy physical and emotional burdens on their often shortened lives. A very large number of the survivors of the battle and the following imprisonment suffered emotional trauma and malnutrition-induced health problems long after the war ended. The story of the struggle of those who returned to Canada to try to live a normal life is not within the scope of this book, but most of their lives were shortened, distorted, and debilitated by their experience. No one who survived to return after the ordeal escaped the emotional and physical trauma of the Battle of Hong Kong and the starvation, malnutrition, slave labour, anxiety, and humiliation suffered in Japanese prison camps.

The decision of the Canadian Cabinet under Prime Minister Mackenzie King to send Canadians to Hong Kong was incomprehensible. They did not correctly assess the strategic situation in the Far East, under the growing menace of Japan's belligerence. They showed no concern for the actual military situation in the Far East and Hong Kong until the entire Canadian force had disappeared in the flaming wreckage of the defeated colony. General Henry Crerar, Canada's senior military officer and a man who spent his life as a professional soldier, should have advised against such utter folly. Why he did not is still unexplained.

The Duff Royal Commission, appointed by Mackenzie King (at the insistence of the Opposition in Parliament) to inquire into the reasons for the catastrophe at Hong Kong, found no one at fault and cheerfully exonerated all those involved. To me, it is ironic that these brave young men should have had their fate determined by such rash negligence. It is interesting to note that, a few months after the debacle at Hong Kong, this same Canadian Cabinet was responsible for the equally tragic, hopeless, and even more costly fiasco at Dieppe, but at least there, after the slaughter on the beaches, some soldiers were evacuated to England.

Chapter Six

Prisoner of War (1942–1945)

Delivered at the last moment from death on the battlefield, we now faced an uncertain future and a new challenge — how to survive at the hands of our brutal captors.

On the 30th of December, we were marched across the island from Stanley to North Point, on the northeastern shore of the island. North Point had been a Chinese refugee centre before the war and was now to serve as our prison camp. Nearly four years of starvation, maltreatment, and torture were about to begin. As we marched from Stanley Fort to North Point Camp, our guards called a halt to the marching column near Lye Mun, very close to where the main Japanese force had come ashore. As we sat resting beside the road, a blood-stained covered, dishevelled figure tottered up and asked to join us. Where had he been? He told us he was a cook's helper in the Royal Rifles and was working with Sergeant Cook Gary Cousins, preparing food at Lye Mun, when the Japanese invaders broke into their kitchen. All day they were forced to unload ammunition from Japanese landing barges and carry it ashore. As the sun began to set, they were both lined up on the road beside a deep ditch, hands tied behind their backs, and bayonetted. They fell into the ditch and were left for dead.

When the assistant cook regained consciousness, it was still dark and he found he was lying under Sergeant Cousins's corpse. His wounds had stopped bleeding and by some miracle, the bayonet thrusts had missed his vital organs. He was in pain but he found he could move. Somehow he worked his hands free of their bonds. After a long and painful struggle, he extracted himself from under his dead sergeant and cautiously peered over the edge of the ditch. The road above him was occupied by Japanese reinforcements marching in haste to support their forward elements of the battle. At last a break in the traffic occurred and he was able to crawl away from the ditch and distance himself from the road. He was covered with blood, dressed only in his light fatigues, had no food, and by now was desperate for water. On all fours, he crawled away from the road until he came upon a heavily built steel and concrete shelter with a massive steel door that had been used to protect C Company personnel from Japanese shellfire. He crawled inside, closed and bolted the door, and passed out again. When he came to, he began to explore his self-imposed dungeon in pitch darkness. He discovered that its past occupants had left him half a package of army biscuits, a container of water, and a large jar of rum. What to do? He was now behind Japanese lines, he knew of the danger of infection to his four deep wounds, he had food and water perhaps for two or three days at the most, and the rum. If he unbolted the massive door and was discovered, he knew he would be summarily executed by the Japanese but, on the other hand, if he remained in his present sanctuary it would very soon become not only his hiding place but his tomb. He lay in the dark, slipping in and out of consciousness, until he lost all track of time. Suddenly, he was awakened by a fierce rattling and heavy thuds to the door. A Japanese mop-up force was at the shelter. They attempted for about half an hour to batter down the door, with no success. The door held.

Later, perhaps a day or so later, he was awakened by an explosion — someone was trying to blast their way into the shelter — but again the door held. After being holed up in the shelter for about 11 days, the pangs of hunger and thirst drove him to open the door to begin a desperate search for food and water. When he opened the door, it was broad daylight, and as he crept out of the shelter and closer to the road, he heard the unmistakable sound of the English language. He crept closer still until he could see a long line of unarmed khaki-clad Canadian soldiers resting by the side of the road. He survived the bayonetting, and the Japanese prison camps, and, nearly four years later, he made it home with his scars to support his incredible story.

North Point Prison Camp.

North Point Camp had been a battleground where the Japanese had initially landed, and it was littered with the dead and decomposing bodies of men and pack animals. The litter, filth, and stench of the dead were awful and made a perfect breeding place for millions of flies. The huts were riddled with shrapnel and there was no running water, no latrines, no cooking facilities, and no food or water for the prisoners. The ground was ploughed up by shellfire and covered with the wreckage of the battle.

Upon arrival, the men, many of them walking wounded and all of them exhausted, simply lay on the ground or on the cement floor of the shattered, windowless huts. The crowding of the facilities, such as they were, made for hopeless congestion. Lice, fleas, and bedbugs were rampant. There was no soap and not even the simplest items of hygiene, such as toothbrushes, were available.

The men were filthy and battle-stained. Within a short time, many were infected by the cloud of disease-carrying flies and began to succumb to a virulent form of amoebic dysentery. There were no medical supplies, no hospital, and no provisions for the sick and the wounded. The seriously wounded and the dysentery cases lay on their stretchers where we had carried them. They were now covered with their own blood and filth and crawling with flies. This was our introduction to a Japanese camp and to how the Japanese treated their prisoners.

When food was finally issued the next day, it consisted of mouldy rice full of rat droppings and worms. Our rations were two bowls of rice per day, one in the morning and one in the evening, and one sourdough bun per man, at noon. Nutritionists have calculated that in order to maintain health and weight, a soldier or an average male engaged in manual labour requires 3,500 calories per day. It is estimated that at North Point Camp, where the diet consisted almost entirely of rice and chrysanthemum tops, the caloric intake for the individual prisoner was about 1,200 calories. Added to the lack of calories in the daily diet was the severe deficiency of essential vitamins such as the B complex, so essential to maintaining health. Lieutenant-Colonel Sutcliffe, commanding officer of the Grenadiers, was the first to die of malnutrition in these appalling conditions. He was soon followed by many others.

Sergeant Lance Ross, my fellow sergeant in D Company, at great risk to himself kept a secret diary. Here are some of the entries he made at North Point:

Jan. 2, 1942	Very fine day. The stench is terrible. We put ground over some of the bodies.
Feb. 13	We are almost frozen and our roof leaks awful.
Feb. 16	Dysentery is widespread throughout the camp.
Feb. 18	I believe we are going to starve to death.
Feb. 22	We are terribly hungry. Just talk about food.
March 1	We are getting lousy as coots. We are crowded so close together.
March 23	Rice and water three times a day.
April 20	Hitler's birthday, also Aunt Bessie's. Many more to her.
May 14	Japanese knocked out a Chinese and left him on the street (outside the camp) in rain all day. Just before dark bayonetted him; he was alive this morning.
May 16	Japanese have two Chinese women tied to a post. They have shot their husbands.

May 25	Heat getting bad, 110 degrees in shade. Mosquitoes eating us alive.
June 13	Japanese say they attacked Aleutians. Bedbugs getting worse.
June 30	Food is awful. Rice in morning — bun dinner — some kind of greens like weeds.
July 14	Heavy rain all night. Sleep outdoors on concrete so many bugs.
Aug. 12	Man died. Many going blind — gradually getting weaker.
Aug. 16	Conditions getting unbearable, we will all die in this terrible place.
Aug. 27	Hot, 100 degrees in shade. Two men died last night.
Sept. 1	Rain and mud. First man of my section died with dysentery.
Sept. 11	More men falling sick every day.
Sept. 12	Another died today, we wrapped him in a sheet, buried him across the road.
Sept. 14	Another death in my platoon, pneumonia.
Sept. 19	Very hot. Men dying at rate of three a day, malaria, dysentery, fever.
Sept. 21	More sick, some going blind. Three died today.
Sept. 26	Went to Shamshuipo. The barracks are bombed and shelled, not a window left.

As I set down these recollections of our prison-camp experience, I wonder now that any of us survived. At North Point we knew that we were slowly starving to death, but we also knew that a bout of amoebic dysentery would speed up the process and almost certainly guarantee a very unpleasant death. Geoffrey C. Marston, a member of the Royal Rifles, recalled his bout with dysentery at North Point Camp as follows:

> In the second week of July 1942 with the rain pelting down I was experiencing persistent bowel movements followed by extreme stomach cramps, nausea and weakness. At first I thought it was a bad case of diarrhea caused by intestinal disorders due to the terrible diet that we had to endure. But I was wrong. Not long afterwards I noticed my stool streaked with blood and mucous and realized the dread dysentery was racking my body.... Committed to the camp's ramshackle hospital which reeked with undescribable stench, I was helped to a cot and lay huddled on it, wet with rain that was seeping through the rotten roof. Next to me lay a very young-looking comrade who was labouring for breath. I was certain he was deteriorating more and more into a state of no return....
>
> The atmosphere was frightening. Patients were tottering at a snail's pace along a narrow aisleway to reach a closed-in quarter at the end of the ward that was used as a toilet. Those unable to muster the strength to leave their so-called beds lay in their own muck. Dirty, blood-stained pieces of toilet paper littered the floor.
>
> Mustering enough strength to pay a toilet call I reeled back from the awful stench of the room containing nothing more than five peanut-oil cans that were in constant use, and those who

couldn't control their body functions had to use the floor. Cakes of excrement and pools of urine lay everywhere. The filth proved a mecca for rats who were scampering about in large numbers. We were deathly afraid that they would attack our buttocks, thereby devouring chunks of flesh. Time and again orderlies tried to stave them off with long sticks to keep them from coming near....

In the meantime our officers confronted the Japanese and sternly requested that they repair the decayed roof and provide better toilet facilities but the Japanese were adamant by refusing to do so and declared in anger that if they were further bothered all prisoners would be subjected to a cut in food ration.

The rodents that were swimming around the floating muck tried to clamber onto our beds. Some succeeded and began attacking the flesh of patients. But they didn't feel it. The flesh was dead.

The lad next to me expired. I watched as the orderlies taped his eyes and stuffed his mouth and rectum with cotton wool and wrapped the remains in a blanket, then placed it on a stretcher and took it away. Our overworked doctors and orderlies worked feverishly almost around the clock trying to save those who were still clinging to a shred of life. Without any source of medication their only alternative to combat the disease was no intake of food for several days to stabilize the intestines. Only tea was given several times daily. Our padres spent every minute of their time trying to comfort us.... On the third day I could feel my strength rapidly declining. I could not raise myself off the bed. I was growing weaker and weaker. The room was spinning like a top with the sounds around me gradually diminishing.

Rifleman Marston was one of those few who recovered and was later shipped to Japan where he survived the war, his weight falling to 92 pounds before his release in northern Japan in September 1945.

Escape seemed impossible because of our inability to speak Chinese, our inability to merge with the population, and our lack of water transportation. Despite these obstacles, on August 19, 1942, a sergeant and three riflemen escaped from the camp. They were quickly recaptured and tortured for a week in front of Colonel Tokunaga and then beheaded. Their remains have never been found.

In September of 1942, after nine months in this hellhole, we were moved from North Point Camp on the island to Shamshuipo Camp on the mainland. Here the crowding was less of a problem, but now we were forced to work every day with pick and shovel at lengthening the runways of the Kai Tak Airport, with no improvement in rations. It was here that we were exposed to the notorious "Kamloops Kid." He was an interpreter for the Japanese who had been born in Kamloops, British Columbia, of Japanese parents, and moved to Japan before the war. His name was Kanao Inouye and he was charged with torture resulting in the deaths of four men and one woman. Inouye described his "favourite" tortures to his interrogators as the "water torture," the "flying airplane," and the "hanging torture." He was a sadistic maniac who vented his sickness in the deliberate torture and abuse of his Canadian countrymen. By now I had been promoted to Warrant Officer II and I stood by in helpless fury as I watched him abuse my men. At the end of the war, he was captured at Hong Kong, tried, and executed by an Allied court for his conduct at Shamshuipo.

It was at Shamshuipo that an outbreak of diphtheria added to the scourge of dysentery, malaria, and malnutrition. In October 1942, diphtheria raged among the prisoners in an epidemic that lasted for six months. At its height, men died every day, and by the end of this period another 54 men in our regiment had needlessly died of a combination of malnutrition and diphtheria. The Japanese refused to supply serum to fight the disease and showed a callous indifference to our doctors' repeated pleas for some, or any, form of medication for those afflicted. Instead of providing serum or some form of assistance to our doctors, Dr. Saito, the ranking Japanese medical officer, accused our doctors and orderlies of neglecting their patients, for which they were beaten.

By now, after more than 16 months of captivity, almost every prisoner suffered from beriberi, dysentery, partial blindness, pellagra, tropical ulcers, and serious skin infections. Added to these afflictions was "electric feet," caused by malnutrition, in which the victim experienced a pain like that of multiple needles being plunged into his flesh night and day, without relief. Dr. Stanley Banfill, a medical officer of the Royal Rifles, remembered his experience in Shamshuipo as follows:

> The first four months after our move (to Shamshuipo), September '42 to January '43, were the most difficult and depressing of our imprisonment. I think the chief factors that made this so were forced labour, malnutrition and the diphtheria epidemic.
>
> The Japanese were engaged in clearing away the debris of war and were lengthening the landing strip at Kai Tak.... The Japanese demanded a certain number of men each day and set the

quota high. Eventually it became clear even to our captors that they were asking the impossible of sick and exhausted men and the work parties were discontinued.

The food was inadequate in both amount and kind. Rice and greens (green horror) with hardly any fats and an occasional minute ration of fish was near starvation to us. As a result we developed severe malnutrition and this aggravated the tropical diseases and those spread by our crowding that now hit us....

The result was disastrous as 74 Canadians developed diphtheria before we could get any antitoxin and of these 54 died. When we started having several deaths a day the Japanese became alarmed. Possibly the disease was spreading to their troops and their seniors demanded action. They began swabbing throats to detect carriers and insisted everyone on pain of punishment wear a face mask day and night.

They showed their fear of criticism by ordering that diphtheria should not appear as the cause of death on our reports and, most surprising, Dr. Saito (chief medical officer for all Hong Kong prisoner-of-war camps) lined up all medical personnel, mostly devoted volunteer orderlies, and slapped their faces for permitting their patients to die.... Our physical ailments were mostly due to malnutrition and could only have been treated adequately with good food. We had every known deficiency disease except scurvy. Everyone suffered from some degree of beri-beri and pellagra and we saw all of their unpleasant manifestations — the severe sleep-robbing pain of "hot foot" was almost unbearable to the victim and increasing, and sometimes sudden, blindness seemed to forecast a hopeless future. We also had the common tropical diseases whose effect was exaggerated in men suffering from malnutrition.... Tropical ulcers were common and parasitic infestation was universal.

Those who could not stand the psychological and emotional shock of these conditions and the starvation tactics and studied brutality of our captors soon died to escape what, for them, was intolerable. They were a small minority. For the rest, we maintained strict discipline. Daily orders and crime sheets for disobedience of any orders were in effect. We were an organized military unit, with its formal structure and ranks intact and fully operational. No unit was left outside this formal, regimented organization, and each individual was constantly reminded that he was a Canadian soldier who was only temporarily under the control of the Japanese. I have no doubt that this discipline and philosophy saved countless lives and provided concrete support for the survival of many who would otherwise have died. The will to live is very strong. The desire not to disgrace your uniform or to let your officers and comrades down through personal weakness is just as strong.

The worse the conditions got, the more determined I was that I would not crack. I would not admit to any weakness and I would always present a cheerful, optimistic front to my men. Above all, I was determined that we would live to see the inevitable Allied victory, no matter what.

Under these conditions, the men of the Royal Rifles were magnificent, and as a whole they again showed their courage, their spirit, and their strength.

A great deal has been written about the cruelty of the Japanese towards their prisoners. To me, Japanese cruelty could not be exaggerated. I personally witnessed their actual behaviour and they were savage in the extreme. Once aroused, they behaved with no restraint — like madmen. However, I found in the private soldiers themselves, especially if they were combat troops, out of sight of their officers, little of this ferocity and cruelty. In fact, they sometimes turned a blind eye to prisoners' infractions of the rules, which, if discovered, would have enraged their superiors. They said often, and I believed them, that they hated the war as much as we did.

During the diphtheria epidemic at Shamshuipo, a Japanese military interpreter, who in peacetime was a Christian minister, smuggled into the camp against orders a large amount of diphtheria serum that saved hundreds of lives. He was discovered, arrested, and court-martialled. No doubt he was executed for his "crime."

In 1943, the Japanese began shipping prisoners of war from Hong Kong to Japan to work as slave labour. On January 19 of that year, I was sent on a draft to Japan with 663 of our men from Shamshuipo. We embarked in Hong Kong Harbour on the Japanese vessel *Tatuta Maru* for our run through the American-submarine–infested waters of the China Sea, on our way to Nagasaki in the south of Japan.

We were battened down in a cargo hold below the waterline. The hold was so crowded that only half of its occupants could lie down at one time. There were no sanitary facilities in the hold except for some odious buckets that served this purpose, and the temperature soared to one hundred degrees. Thus began a nightmare journey, with a large number of the men suffering from dysentery. Rice balls and water were passed down twice daily from the deck above and our latrine buckets were emptied once per day.

The draft before us, made up of British prisoners sailing on the unmarked Japanese ship *Lisbon Maru*, had been torpedoed and sunk by an American submarine, with fearful loss of life when the Japanese abandoned the ship, leaving their prisoners to drown below deck under battened-down hatches. Those who escaped drowning were machine-gunned in the water by Japanese escort ships and, of these, only a handful escaped by playing dead. They were then rescued at dawn the next day by Chinese fishermen. Fifteen hundred PoWs died.

At the end of this claustrophobic week, we docked at Nagasaki and staggered out of the hold onto the freezing Nagasaki docks, filthy beyond belief. Some of the men were caked with their own excrement and all were barely able to walk. We were met by one of the Emperor's elite guard regiments, who were to be our escorts on the train to our destination at Yokohama. They were visibly shocked at our condition and did their best to clean us up before boarding the train. Once on the train, pots of tea were served with meals in individual boxes containing rice, pickles, pork, and vegetables. I can still hear them sucking in their breath against their teeth in a typical Japanese gesture of disgust as they examined their filthy, starving charges. They did everything they could for us, and we were fed again at each stop until we reached Camp 3D at Kawasaki, a suburb of Yokohama.

This camp was a hastily erected wooden structure with outside walls made of half-inch plywood. Canadian chicken coops were built with more concern for their occupants. Inside these huts were raised sleeping shelves covered by woven bamboo mats. As the summer waned and the winter of Japan came upon us, the huts were damp and freezing cold. The two wooden fibre blankets issued to us were inadequate, and we suffered now not only from insufficient calories but also from the unrelenting cold in these shoddy, porous boxes.

We were sent to work in the Nippon Kokan shipyard, building ships for the Japanese merchant marine. Out of each 14-day period, we worked 13 days and rested one. We were issued with flimsy work uniforms with our numbers on them. I was *nanobon* (number seven).

The amount and quality of the rations were still completely inadequate and our malnutrition continued. After another year of this regime, I became little more than a listless, tottering six-foot-four skeleton, unable to work, but hanging grimly onto life and praying, seemingly in vain, for a speedy Allied victory over Japan.

I was forced to tramp out to the shipyard every morning with my comrades of the work gang where I was turned over to the civilian foreman who was responsible for my work. He could see I was unable to work and was slowly dying of malnutrition. He would suck in his breath over his teeth and ask me (using the Japanese word for "head man") "*Hancho*, what can we do?" Finally, having failed at every job he gave me because I simply could not keep up, he gave me assignments that required a minimum of effort. At the first, tucked away out of the sight of patrolling guards, he had me sit on a little stool and scrape rust from large used bolts with a stiff wire brush. Another job he gave me was to sit before a large ship's boiler and slide condenser rods one at a time into pre-cut holes. Finally, to keep me more visibly busy to the guards, he had me paint, with a long-handled paint-brush, the white aisle demarcation stripes on the factory floor, with carbide sludge. Each day at the shipyard where I was forced to go through the motions of work seemed as if it would never end. The winters were the worst. Japan is bitterly cold and damp in the winter months and because we had insufficient calories and inadequate, worn-out clothing that provided insufficient protection from the cold, we suffered continuously from the winter temperatures. There was no escape from the cold, either in the camp nor in the miserable, freezing work sheds of the shipyard where I was confined during the day. To keep from going mad, I tried to escape the misery of the present by daydreaming. I tried to free my mind from my starving, often lice-covered body by letting it soar back across the blue Pacific to Canada and to the warm, carefree, sunlit days of my boyhood. I tried to relive my life with my wonderful mother and my father. I relived our Christmas mornings, our picnics and our beach parties to Wascana Lake, and all the joyous experiences I had shared with my parents, grandparents, uncles and aunts, cousins, and friends at home. Somehow, the paralytic minutes and hours ticked by and another day of captivity was over and, at dawn, another day began. And, as it will, each day passed yet again into another day.

1943 Japanese records photo.

How long, I wondered, will it be before our rescuers come, and how long can I avoid being the subject of the next hasty funeral in the dark at the camp, accompanied by the eerie sound of the attending Shinto priest's bells? But, like my comrades, I walked again and yet again on the treadmill to the shipyard and never gave up hope. From time to time, my unsuspecting foreman assigned me to another easy job at the shipyard, that of filling the grease reservoirs over ships' engine bearings. These reservoirs were made of brass, had a spring-loaded cover, and were called grease caps. Despite the misery and the growing despair of our situation, I never missed an opportunity, when undetected, to first fill the grease caps with iron filings before filling the rest of the cap with thick grease. Once the ship was at sea, the heat of the engine would slowly liquefy the grease in the cap, the iron filings would begin to lacerate the babbitt lining of the bearing, and soon the bearing would burn out. This was a very dangerous pastime and would have been fatal had I been caught, but the Canadian prisoners at the Nippon Kokan, while forced to work, never ceased to find ways to sabotage and frustrate the Japanese shipbuilding effort. We were not an asset to Japanese war production and had no plans to be one.

My fellow prisoners worked in various other heavy jobs in the shipyard, including rivetting on the ships, under their respective foremen. We became adept thieves and black-market operators who would sell and trade anything for food, which when received would be wolfed down on the spot. While my foreman looked the other way, I gathered from the floor of the workers' cafeteria orange peels and other edible leftovers. This was a humiliating experience, but I swallowed my pride with the orange peels. Our black-market dealings sometimes led to painful beatings and even death, for Japanese civilians and prisoners alike. On June 22, 1944, Private Baraskovitch of the Winnipeg Grenadiers was accused of stealing a small can of salmon at the shipyard.

Baraskovitch was in my section and when he was taken to the guardroom for questioning, I accompanied him to defend him and plead his innocence. The Japanese soon determined that he was guilty and that I was lying to save him. They became angrier and angrier, and they began to scream and work themselves into a fury, slapping, punching, and kicking us at random. Then, with our hands tied to an iron grating above our heads, we were beaten with three-foot staves about two inches in diameter. Baraskovitch was so badly beaten that he was maimed for life and required an operation when he was freed. I was beaten, also so badly, in fact, that I was unable to work for days and passed a lot of blood from what was feared to be damaged kidneys. After the war, the three Japanese guards, Privates Yamanaka, Shibata, and Baba, all were tried, convicted, and sentenced to long prison terms for this violent assault upon Baraskovitch and me.

Filthy and never quite free from lice, we staggered on as one day led to another, one month led to another, and winter gave way to spring and then to summer. All the while, my men were dying one at a time, to be cremated after a Shinto funeral held at night after work. During our stay at Camp 3D, a further 26 men died of malnutrition and its associated conditions. However, there were lighter moments as the spirit and sense of humour of these gutsy Quebeckers came to the fore.

Soon after we arrived at Camp 3D in Yokohama, the Japanese general in overall command of the Japanese prison camps came with his retinue to the camp to give us a speech. He was a big fat Japanese in his olive dress uniform, polished boots, gold braid, and a great samurai sword trailing in its inlaid scabbard at his side. He was an imposing figure, oozing authority, as he swaggered into the camp to inspect the guard and then to address the assembled prisoners. He climbed up on a box placed in the centre of the parade ground before us and launched, scowling at us all the while, into a diatribe in Japanese that his interpreter translated for us. He told us we were prisoners and lucky to be allowed to live. We could, and would, be summarily executed for any disobedience to the soldiers of the Emperor. Japan was winning the war on every front and would soon invade our homeland and subject Canada to Japanese rule. After that occurred and perhaps after 20 years, we may be allowed to go home. We were slaves with no rights, no hope for anything better, and no prospects. As these doleful words were spoken by this scowling, brutal figure, I preferred to think of the growing power of the advancing Allied armed forces and to wonder if this man really believed in the nonsense he spoke.

Captain John Reid, Canadian medical officer.

We were dismissed and, slowly and quietly, we went back to sit on our bed shelves in our huts. Within minutes, one of our French-Canadian riflemen, who was a born mimic and comedian, rose on a bed in the centre of the hut to command our attention. He soon had us roaring with laughter, as in the arrogant gestures of the general and in the comical broken English of the Japanese interpreter, he did his impressions of them. In a perfect imitation of the general, he gave us his speech in what he pretended was Japanese, scowling all the while and pausing for effect. And then he interpreted his own speech in the broken English of the interpreter: Japan was losing the war; he was sorry for all the mistakes they had made; he had come to apologize for the bad food and accommodations; he was sorry we had sabotaged so many of his ships, but he could understand our annoyance; and so on! The hut rocked with laughter as we saw in that flash of humour the general for what he was — a blustering, brutal bully. He knew Japan was losing the war and to bolster his sagging ego, he was intimidating a group of men systematically being starved to death. His samurai sword, dragging at his side, was symbolic of his backward warrior class, wreaking misery on us and the poor people of Japan. Later that day, our medical officer, Captain John Reid, was summoned by the camp commandant to explain why, in the face of these awful threats and this intimidating message, we had reacted with such mirth. What kind of people were we anyway? How could there be anything to laugh at? Were we insane? No, we were Canadians, and we were going to resist to the very end, whatever that end might be!

At Camp 3D, there were some events that stand out in my memory. On October 4, 1944, the air-raid sirens sounded their warning for the first time, on a beautiful, clear fall day. All of the workers in the shipyard, including the prisoners, ran outside to stare up at the cloudless sky. There, at 35,000 feet, the sunlight glinting and sparkling from its reflective aluminum skin like a silver ghost, was a giant American bomber leisurely photographing

Japan at an altitude that Japanese fighters, try as they might, could not reach. This was the B29, the biggest bomber ever built, and based eight hours flight away in newly acquired American bases in the Mariana Islands. We saw this day the very first evidence that we were not alone. The Allied forces had not been defeated, as we were repeatedly told by the Japanese, and before our very eyes, high above Japan, was the visible evidence of American military reach and power. The presence of this bomber, however, produced another problem in that no doubt the shipyard where we worked every day would be a primary target when the bombing began. It would be like working on a bull's eye at a shooting range.

In the fall of 1944, the Japanese issued us each with a Red Cross parcel. It contained 22 pounds of valuable nutrients to supplement our meagre diet. This, to many of us, was evidence that as their military situation worsened, our captors were reconsidering their decision to work and starve us to death without concern. At any rate, this gave us a tremendous lift, and no doubt saved many men who would have died that winter.

In March of 1945, just as the high-altitude bombing of Japan intensified, the U.S. Air Force located at Guam and the Mariana Islands changed their bombing strategy for Japan. Instead of attempting high-altitude pinpoint bombing of specific targets such as an aircraft factory with high explosives, they decided to drop incendiaries on the closely packed wooden and paper houses of the major cities of Japan. These became known as the great "fire raids" that struck terror into the Japanese. As we were close by at Kawasaki-Yokohama at Camp 3D, we witnessed this fiery holocaust. The first of these raids occurred on the night of March 9–10. Three hundred forty-six giant B29 bombers flew in from the sea at an altitude of only five thousand feet to bomb Tokyo. Their mission was to drop 60 tons of incendiary bombs per square mile of the city and burn out the city's residential heart. As the wind that night was from the west, the bombers began their low-altitude runs of the city from east to west, and as each plane reached its aiming point, it began to unload its seven tons of M69 incendiaries. The heat from one of these bombs could melt concrete. The Japanese night fighters and anti-aircraft guns were taken completely by surprise, having expected bombing above 20,000 feet. Thus there was far less resistance from the Tokyo anti-aircraft and fighters' defences than had been expected and only 12 American aircraft failed to return to their base.

By 2:00 a.m. on the morning of March 10, Tokyo was a flaming inferno. The closely packed residential areas of light wooden and paper structures were engulfed in flames. As the fire intensified, it created a need for oxygen at its base, and a raging firestorm developed that swept parts of buildings, objects of every kind, and even people into its incandescent maw. The fire was so intense that not only was Tokyo's fire department rendered virtually useless but 98 of its heavy fire trucks soon became flaming,

American B29 Superfortress.

melting wrecks. Six hundred of its firemen simply disappeared. The loss of life to the Japanese civilians in the city was horrific. It is estimated that more than 100,000 Japanese residents of Tokyo were incinerated that night. Two hundred sixty-one thousand homes were destroyed, leaving 1.15 million homeless. The next day, American photo reconnaissance planes confirmed that 15.8 square miles of Tokyo had been reduced to ashes.

But this was only the beginning of the payback for Pearl Harbor. The B29s came back again on April 13 and on April 15 they bombed Kawasaki, the site of our prison camp. They came back again on May 23, May 25, and attacked Yokohama on May 29. By now the Japanese air defences were reeling and their effectiveness was substantially reduced as American bombers bombed at will, with less and less resistance. Before the B29s were through with the Tokyo urban area, Japanese civilian casualties numbered 216,988; 713,366 dwellings were destroyed and 56.3 square miles of the urban area of Tokyo had been reduced to ashes. As we prisoners watched this fiery destruction unfold before our eyes, we knew the Allies were closing the ring around Japan and that the Japanese could not stand these crippling assaults for long — but for how long? As we watched the growing power of the U.S. Air Force, our hopes were raised, but could we escape the coming showdown as we watched the tongues of fire lapping even to the edge of our camp? Now that end was coming near, would we live to see it?

As if the firebombing of the residential areas of Tokyo were not enough, the Canadian prisoners of war at the Nippon Kokan shipyards, Japan's largest shipbuilder, had a plan of their own to add some serious damage to Tokyo's industrial sector as well. Under the secret and skilful direction of Staff Sergeant Charlie Clark of Brigade Headquarters, in the dead of night when the prisoners were back in their camp, mysterious fires broke out simultaneously under the massive blueprint library and the pattern warehouse. These fires were started by ingenious delayed fuses manufactured by the prisoners and fed by carefully planted inflammatory materials. Since this was long before the electronic storage of such data was possible, it brought ship construction to a grinding halt. These fires, set by Clark and his daring plotters, did more damage to that shipyard than all the B29 raids on it of the entire war.

The Japanese were furious as it was not only an economic blow and production loss of great significance to the war effort, but it was a massive loss of face as well. Somebody or some group would have to be blamed and executed for this sabotage. I thought I was a member of a small group who were sure to be blamed. Wisely, Clark told no one, including me, of their plan and thus insulated everyone but the actual perpetrators from the possibility of a leak under torture. The Japanese camp commander suspected the prisoners of Camp 3D, of course, but if his hunch was correct and he could prove it, he also knew he would be held accountable by his superiors for the disaster since the prisoners were entirely under his control. He would be disgraced and ruined, if not hanged, by a miliary court. We were questioned but, thanks to Clark's secrecy, we knew absolutely nothing about the sabotage and convincingly said so. After a while, the matter died down and we still don't know how our camp commandant escaped the noose or how the fires were explained but quite possibly, in collusion with shipyard officials, the fires were blamed on one of the nightly B29 bombing raids.

This act of defiance was another example of the sheer guts and spirit of the Canadians. After more than three years of starvation, sickness, slavery, and humiliation, their spirit of resistance and their loyalty to their cause was undiminished. They knew the risks but they also knew that if they could, their duty was to cripple Japanese ship production. Courage on the battlefield in the heat of an action is one thing, but to coolly and calmly plot and carry out these acts of sabotage, knowing full well the awful consequences of discovery, called for courage of another kind entirely. The sheer audacity of this action in the centre of the enemy's homeland, right under their noses, was amazing. Long after, when I congratulated Clark for his actions, he smiled and said, "It went rather well, didn't it?"

As a prisoner of war I met some fascinating soldiers, sailors, and airmen from other countries who had also fallen into the hands of the Japanese. There was a Dutch submarine crew whose sub was sunk in the Bay of Tonkin. I met a group of tough Australians and some British from the Royal Air Force stationed in Singapore. There were American sailors who had survived the naval battle in the Sunda Strait and American soldiers from the Philippines, all caught in the deadly net cast by the sudden onslaught of the Japanese conquest of Southeast Asia.

One of these characters was an officer of the United States Navy. One day in the winter of 1944, while we were in Yokohama in Camp 3D, I learned that a high-ranking Allied officer was coming to stay at the camp. That afternoon, a Japanese staff car drove up and from it emerged a very senior American naval officer, immaculately attired in navy dress blues. He wore a matching blue naval overcoat over his uniform and he looked as if he had just stepped off the quarterdeck of a battleship. His sleeves were adorned with the multiple gold rings of his rank and he had a wreath of gold scrambled eggs on the peak of his impressive hat. He was a small man, about 50 years old, and he stood ramrod straight. He gazed straight ahead, as if his eyes were fixed on some very distant object. He gave no sign of recognition, either to those who accompanied him in the car or to the Japanese reception committee at the gate. When he proceeded to enter the gate, the guards backed up quickly and scrambled around him, out to the car to get his suitcase and sea bag — I noticed that he never attempted to carry his own bag. He stalked into the camp as if he were sleepwalking through an annoying dream and disappeared into the hut, where he was given a small private room with a small bed, desk, and chair. Seldom did he come out of his cubbyhole.

He ate his rice and barley in his cubicle and refused to work or even walk out to the shipyard. He flatly refused to parade for roll call and ignored the Japanese. He did not speak. He seemed unwilling or unable to accept his surroundings and it was apparent that while his body was with us, his mind was elsewhere. He was a very, very angry man, brooding on his fate.

Months went by and once in a while he was seen fully dressed in his impressive blue uniform with the gold braid, walking around the parade ground, staring straight ahead, acknowledging no one, and uttering not a single word. One day, I asked the other U.S. naval officer in the camp about this mysterious naval person. He said, "He was captured by the Japanese in the Philippines, where he was commandant of the naval dockyard in Manila." I then asked him, "Why is he so silent?" He replied, "He was a graduate of Annapolis, and his classmates, including Ernest J. King, commander of all U.S. naval operations, are now admirals commanding the massive U.S. Navy at sea." These men had received many promotions since the start of the war with Japan because of the build-up of naval forces and he was completely out of the picture as a career naval officer. He had spent his life preparing to command U.S. naval forces at sea and, instead, here he sat while all his Annapolis classmates were rising rapidly in rank in the mighty U.S. Navy. He was furious at his fate and could not unbend or adjust to his circumstances. Everybody in our camp, including the Japanese, watched with respect as he strode by and no one wanted to interrupt or antagonize this silent, forbidding figure. I certainly didn't.

One day, months later, he asked to walk out to our workplace with the work party. I was so sick that day my foreman told me to go to the little hut where the prisoners ate their rice and lie down. When I reached the hut, he was staring fixedly out its single, little window. He never spoke or even saw me, I thought, and of course I did not speak to him. After I had lain down on a wooden bench for half an hour or so, I heard a deep voice speaking to me. He said,

"MacDonell, can you imagine me sitting here in this godforsaken hole, surrounded by these bloody people, while in Washington Ernie King is running the whole navy show?" I replied, "No, sir." "What makes me so mad," he said, "is that I am the prisoner of one of the most backward races in the world. Here I sit, missing the whole war in the hands of these people! Let me tell you just how stupid they really are; they can't even make paint!" "Paint?" I said. "Yes," he said, "they can't even make paint." He continued, "Years ago, when I was on shore duty in San Diego, my wife wanted me to paint our toilet seat in our only bathroom. I went to the store and bought a can of paint for the job. I painted the seat but the paint never dried. It was paint made in Japan."

As far as I know, that was one of the only times he ever spoke in captivity. He, of the elite of American naval officers, had been in the wrong place at the wrong time — c'est la guerre! I later learned that he survived both the war and his bad luck and, on the day after his rescue, to Ernie King's credit, he was promoted one full grade in rank.

In May, with great areas of Tokyo and Yokohama turned into smouldering rubble and the shipyard out of action, some 90 of us were suddenly moved to Ohasi Camp in northern Japan, just a few miles north of the port of Kamaishi. The Ohasi camp was a small, remote camp in the mountains that provided labour for mining ore in a nearby iron mine. The iron ore was shipped by a small railway to smelters in Kamaishi. If anything, the misery of working in the shipyard at Yokohama was increased by the necessity to labour underground in a dangerous, unstable mine. The food was no different and no additional rations were issued for working in these conditions.

The camp workforce consisted of American, British, and Canadian prisoners who were marched daily up to the head of the mine, in much the same work regime as in the shipyard. To my surprise, the Japanese decided I was too weak and far too tall for the low ceilings and confined spaces in the mine, so they put me to work temporarily in the camp kitchen as a kitchen helper. This act undoubtedly saved my life, as I was far beyond any strenuous work of any kind, let alone mining.

In June of that year, I was transferred again from the kitchen to work in the mine machine shop, where I performed any low-skilled or clean-up jobs the foreman assigned to me. By now, as we entered the summer of 1945, the war in Europe was over and even in northern Japan, we could see the growing presence of the U.S. Air Force as it flew its daily missions in broad daylight at will over Japan. Low-flying American fighters looking for targets of opportunity were a constant threat. Any marching formation could easily be mistaken for a Japanese troop column and would quickly bring down a hail of .50 calibre machine-gun fire and bombs from these searching destroyers. It was therefore essential to guards and prisoners alike that we were not caught in the open on the road to the mine. Several times in July and August of that year, we lay under cover for hours in the fields and adjoining ditches as American pilots scoured the landscape from low altitude for targets. These were scary but nonetheless welcome interludes from the drudgery of the mine.

Just a few miles south of our mining camp at Ohasi lay the port city of Kamaishi. It was here the smelters for the ore we mined were located and it was here that the smelted pig iron was loaded onto ships for distribution around Japan. On July 14, a hot summer day, a PoW wood-gathering party from our camp high on a local mountain witnessed an awesome spectacle. They watched from their mountain perch high above the city as the U.S. Navy's battleships *South Dakota*, *Indiana*, and *Massachusetts*, supported by a large fleet, fired 802 16-inch shells into Kamaishi, knocking down one after the other the nine giant smokestacks of the main Kamaishi smelter. Again, on August 9, the American battle fleet returned to fire another 850 16-inch shells into Kamaishi. The destruction of the smelter and a steel mill was total. The aimed delivery of 1,600 16-

inch shells from the American bombardment at sea was clear evidence that not only were American forces masters of Japanese air space, but they could now also sail their mighty navy so close to the Japanese shore unopposed that they could use naval artillery freely on specific shore targets. The shell craters of these projectiles left the surface of the city of Kamaishi resembling a devastated moonscape. Even the most confident of the Japanese military began to see the tightening noose of Allied air and sea power. However, at this time, documentary evidence shows that Japanese military leaders were still confident that they could defeat any Allied force if it tried to land on Japan's fortified coast. They were still determined to defeat the Allies on Japanese soil or die to a man in the attempt.

Unfortunately, according to Earl Jacobson of Montreal, a captured merchant seaman who as a PoW worked in the Kamaishi steel mill, 32 British PoWs were killed when one of these American shells made a direct hit on their air-raid shelter. To save the lives of Japanese civilians, both raids were preceded by American planes that dropped leaflets to warn the population to leave the city before the attacks from the sea began.

In the summer of 1945, we knew the war was going very badly for the Japanese. We also knew that in our present debilitated, starving conditions most of us would not live through the coming winter in the mountains. The last of the physical reserves of even the strongest was used up and our resistance to disease, especially pneumonia, was also non-existent. The American naval blockade was effectively reducing the food imports for Japan, and as the food supply for the Japanese people declined, our already inadequate rations declined even further. The consequences of forced labour, torture, studied brutality, and malnutrition were taking their inevitable toll.

The result of this maltreatment is movingly described in the following diary entries of Tom Forsyth of the Grenadiers from Pipestone, Manitoba:

Dec. 17, 1944   Little Waterhouse of the Royal Rifles died — one of the gamest kids I ever saw. Too small for the heavy work, sick and underweight, he toiled uncomplainingly. Sheer willpower sustained him to the end, when, a veritable walking skeleton, he tottered in from work between two of us. Death came as a merciful release.

Dec. 21   Raining wet, miserable. Sergeant Phillips of the Rifles died today.

Dec. 23   A Rifle and a Grenadier died today.

Jan. 1, 1945   About 3:30 this morning when we were all sound asleep from fatigue in the long bunk shed on the sandy hillside I was awakened by the wrenching creaking sound of straining timbers ... then I heard the awful screams of men crushed and trapped beneath the wreckage.

Jan. 2   I was one of the three men detailed to put the dead men in their coffins (eight of them). It was a cold day, snowing and blowing. We were shivering. They lay stark naked in a row and cold as ice. The coffins, cheap flimsy affairs roughly and crudely made, were too short for the bodies.

April 16   An American named Haglund came into hospital (one small room for 15 beri beri cases). He is a skeleton if I ever saw one. Tonight we were issued cards and told we might write a few words home. Haglund asked me if I would write his card for him. I said certainly! What should I write? He gave me his mother's address and told me to say he was fine and they mustn't worry and to send his love. I hesitated but he begged me to, so I wrote it and hoped his mother would forgive me when she eventually heard the truth.

April 17   Haglund very weak this morning. I raised his head and gave him a mouthful of hot coffee and when he lay back he swallowed once and was gone.

April 21   Robley of the Royal Rifles died today at 10 o'clock. He had beri beri, infected leg, and amoebic dysentery. Total of ninety two PoWs out of 600 have died since we landed in Japan. Out of 300 who were Canadians, 75 have died.

"I Am Going To Stick It Out---"

TO _____ CAMP
DATE April 27th 1944

Dear Aunt and Uncle:

I am writing to tell you that I
am still alive at this date.
I am working every day and
still near Yokahama. I received your letter of August 23
1943, two months ago. My
thoughts are with you contin-
ually and your cheering letters keep me going. Please
say hello to Marie and all
of my friends. Give David and
Helen my special regards.
I am glad my broadcast got
through. I am going to stick it
out to the end, and am certain
that the final results will be
happy ones for us. Love

Cpl. M. George MacDonald

A letter home from Camp 3D.

It seemed ironic to me that as the Allied forces grew stronger and stronger and the possibilities of rescue increased, our chances of survival were diminishing. To those who were near the end of their ability to continue on, it was especially hard to realize that help was coming nearer and nearer and yet for them was still so far away. Another difficulty to be faced was the fact that we suspected the Japanese had orders to kill us all if our rescue by Allied forces seemed likely. We later discovered that in fact each Japanese camp commander had specific written orders to kill all prisoners "by any means at [his] disposal" if their rescue seemed likely.

But, by August 1, 1945, we still lived, we still hoped, and we still clung to our dreams of rescue, freedom, and home. I was determined to hang on. I had lost all feeling below the waist and was down to 148 pounds and I knew my chances of survival grew less and less each day, but I also knew there was still a chance!

Chapter Seven

Japanese Surrender and Rescue

On August 1, 1945, Japan was being bombed into ashes and rubble. Oil and other fuel reserves were almost entirely gone and food supplies for its island population were rapidly diminishing as the American Navy tightened its blockade.

Okinawa, just off the coast of Japan, had fallen and the Japanese air force had been shot out of the sky, while almost the entire Japanese navy rested on the bottom of the ocean. Victorious Russian armies, having played their part in defeating Germany, were massing on the border of Manchuria, preparing for the invasion of Japan. Japan was isolated, severely crippled, and stripped of its means to win the war, but the Japanese were still defiant and still determined to fight to the death. The Japanese army and the Japanese people had lost none of their fanatical loyalty to their Emperor. There was no light at the end of the Japanese tunnel, and if the current military reversals continued, there would soon be no tunnel.

After the war, the United States Strategic Bombing Survey reported that the Japanese economy was in a state of collapse by the summer of 1945. The production of coal, iron ore, rubber, and fertilizer had dropped by an average 90 percent because of the destruction of Japanese merchant shipping and the constant air raids on inland transportation infrastructure. Allied submarines and aircraft had damaged and sunk the Japanese tanker fleet to the extent that Japan's annual requirement of 6.5 million tons of oil per year dwindled to 250,000 tons. Aircraft production fell 80 percent by the end of July 1945. In the face of this clear evidence that Japan could not win a war of attrition with the Western powers, you would think Japan's leaders would yield to the inevitable and sue for peace — but they didn't.

A month earlier in July, at the Potsdam Conference in Germany, Stalin, Churchill, and Truman announced that Japan must accept "unconditional surrender" or face invasion by the armies of the combined Allied forces. The Japanese were insulted and furious at this ultimatum. At a meeting called in early August by the Emperor, the Supreme War Council of Japan categorically rejected the ultimatum from the Allies and refused to surrender. At this meeting, the minister for war said, "Would it not be wondrous for this nation to be destroyed like a beautiful flower?" To him, national suicide was an option preferable to surrender. He was not alone. His views were widely shared by the Japanese army as a matter of honour.

To Allied military planners, Japan presented a serious problem. The Japanese military simply would not give up, and no matter how hopeless their situation, they remained a deadly enemy until nearly each and every one of them was killed. At Guadalcanal, New Georgia, New Guinea, and Kiska, Japanese garrisons fought to the end with a fatality rate of 99 percent. Those who were captured alive were wounded and unable to commit suicide. On Okinawa in April of 1945, the Japanese garrison consisted of 76,000 trained combat soldiers. When the battle for Okinawa was over, all 76,000 of them had died fighting. Combined casualties for the U.S. Army, Navy, and Marines were 72,358. If the American forces had suffered more than 72,000 casualties from 76,000 Japanese defenders at Okinawa, almost one for one, what would American casualties be when they tried to invade Japan? Moreover, the mountainous terrain of Japan favoured the defenders. There were only two locations in Japan where the terrain would allow the deployment of a large invasion force. Both of these, of course, were known to the Japanese and both were fortified in depth against an Allied invasion. Again, because of the terrain, the value of the Allied air power and heavy equipment such as heavy tanks was greatly minimized. Thus, the invasion of Japan would be largely an infantry battle fought face to face with the rifle bullet, the bayonet, and the hand grenade. It was an appalling prospect and a potential bloodbath of monumental proportions. It was estimated that if the Japanese refused to surrender and the Allies forced to invade Japan, Allied army casualties alone would be greater than one million. Japanese casualties would be in the multiple millions if their typical tactics of resistance were employed to defend their sacred homeland, as no doubt they would be.

To meet the threat of an Allied invasion of Japan, the Japanese defence plan, called *Getsu-Go*, included a regular army of 2,903,000 combat soldiers. These would be backed up by a civilian armed militia of some 5 million. Japan also had hoarded and now held ready five thousand Kamikaze planes and pilots to wreak havoc on the ships of an Allied invasion force. The Japanese were absolutely determined to resist the invasion of Japan to the death. Despite the formidable nature of the task, American plans for the invasion of Japan under General Douglas MacArthur were codenamed "Downfall." The first phase, "Olympic," was scheduled to commence with the invasion of southern Japan on November 1, 1945.

So here we were, suspended, facing another winter of starvation and nicely positioned between the hammer and the anvil. It seemed that if we didn't die of starvation, we would be killed deliberately by the Japanese or inadvertently by the invading Allies.

Ohasi Prison Camp.

In August 1945, our camp at Ohasi consisted of approximately 250 prisoners of war, of whom 68 were Canadian survivors of Hong Kong. The camp was completely isolated in the mountains and heavily guarded by regular Japanese troops. We had, carefully hidden in the camp, a secret radio receiver tuned in to the American armed forces broadcast station at San Francisco. This radio was a powerful naval receiving set, salvaged from the American heavy cruiser *Houston* as she was sinking in the Sunda Strait after an outmatched, losing naval battle with the Japanese fleet, early in the war. The *Houston* and other units of the Dutch, Australian, and American western Pacific fleet were all sunk together within a few hours by superior Japanese naval forces. As the signal crew of the sinking *Houston* went over the side into the water, each took a vital component of the ship's radio receiver with him. These components were cleverly hidden in fake water bottles, mess kits, false bottoms of haversacks, clothing, and in hollowed-out compartments in the heels of their shoes. Luckily, the Japanese did not discover these hidden components, and eventually members of the *Houston's* crew, under Chief Petty Officer Jack Feliz, arrived in our camp, much the worse for wear but with the vital radio components still hidden and intact. With additional electrical parts and wire stolen from the mine's electrical shop and secretly powered by the camp's electrical system, we had a clandestine radio receiver that could receive signals from the armed forces' nightly news broadcast from San Francisco to the armed services deployed in the Pacific. However, if the Japanese discovered it, anyone having even the remotest contact with the radio or its broadcasts would be summarily executed. The radio was cleverly hidden in a hollowed-out roof beam and controlled from an adjacent upper bunk by the naval rating that operated it after lights-out each night. Its location continued to escape routine searches of the barracks by our guards. To preserve absolute secrecy, only four people knew of its existence: the operator, RSM Leslie Shore, an American army captain in our camp, and me. The day following each broadcast, the American captain and I would go for a walk around the parade ground and I would receive from him a digest of the news. Of course, I could tell no one!

Thus, I knew that Germany was defeated, the Canadian army in Europe was on its way home, and Hitler was dead. I knew the Americans had captured Okinawa and Iwo Jima and that powerful Allied forces were daily closing in on Japan. I knew the British fleet had joined the awesome American fleet in the Pacific, and together they had utterly destroyed the Japanese navy, including Japan's super-battleship, the *Yamato*. I knew that American, British, Canadian, and Australian armies were beginning to assemble in the Pacific for the final bloody assault on Japan. I assumed the Russians would not be far behind. I also knew that the Japanese would fight to the last man in defence of their homeland. They considered it an honour to die for Japan and the Emperor, as they had at Okinawa and everywhere else the invasion of Japanese possessions had taken place.

I knew that if Allied invasion forces came close to rescuing us, the Japanese would kill us first. Later, captured Japanese documents revealed that Japanese camp commanders indeed had orders to kill their prisoners if their rescue by Allied forces was imminent. I knew that in my current physical condition and because of the ever-worsening food rations, my chances of surviving much longer were slim. I was down to about 140 pounds from my normal weight of 195, was losing my eyesight, was suffering severe malnutrition, and had lost all feeling below the waist. I knew that with so little resistance to disease, the slightest infection would turn into pneumonia or some other fatal condition and I too would find my place in the prisoners' burial ground below the camp, as had so many others.

As I digested this information, I could not see for the life of me how in these circumstances any of us could survive the Allied military holocaust that was about to be unleashed on this little mountainous island. At the same time, I was full of hope and promised my men that we would all be home for Christmas. I never once let anyone see just how hopeless our situation seemed to me. I was 23 years old, my life had just begun, and I didn't want to die in these circumstances. I hoped and prayed that a miracle would save us. Surely the Emperor would not allow the destruction of his entire nation. Surely he was not infected by the same suicidal madness of his generals.

I didn't know it, but very soon a series of events would occur, in a period of nine crucial days from the 6th to the 15th of August, that would change the world forever. These events would determine our fate, the fate of Japan, and indeed would affect the future of all mankind. This course of events would save the lives of millions of Japanese and mean freedom for nearly 100,000 Allied prisoners being held in Japan.

On August 6, our radio reported that American bombers had dropped something called an atomic bomb on a Japanese city to the south of us: Hiroshima. We didn't know what an atomic bomb was, but we knew one bomb had destroyed the entire city.

We closely watched the camp commander and our guards for some reaction. None! They didn't know anything about the destruction of Hiroshima. Was this the face-saving event the Emperor needed to surrender and avoid the coming invasion and certain destruction of Japan and his people?

The Japanese ambassador in Moscow on August 7 met with Molotov, the Soviet foreign minister, and asked him to discuss peace terms for Japan with Britain and the United States.

Molotov summoned the Japanese ambassador on August 9 and told him bluntly that, as of that moment, the USSR was declaring war on Japan. There would be no negotiations with the Americans or the British and any further discussions would take place only after Japan's unconditional surrender.

As this discussion was going on, an American bomber dropped another atomic bomb on Nagasaki, with equally devastating results.[*]

---

[*] Many people have criticized President Truman's decision to drop the atomic bomb on Japan. In doing so, he made the invasion of Japan unnecessary. If the invasion, scheduled for November 1945, had gone ahead, it would have led to the greatest and most appalling slaughter in the history of mankind. Not only did the mountainous terrain of the island favour the defenders, but the powerful army of Japan and its civilian population would have fought to the death. All PoWs held on the island would have been killed. Millions of Japanese civilians and Japanese and Allied soldiers would have died in a gigantic battle of extermination. The battered people of Japan did not deserve that, nor did the weary soldiers, sailors, and marines of the United States.

Now Japan was truly alone and defiantly facing the imminent invasion of the combined Allied armies of the United States, Great Britain, the Soviet Union, Australia, and Canada.

Reeling from these disastrous developments, on August 10 the Japanese informed the Allies through Switzerland that if the Emperor could retain his post as head of state, Japan *may* surrender.

President Truman, on behalf of the Allies, sent a radio message to the Japanese on August 11, informing them that if they surrendered immediately, they could retain the current status of the Emperor.

On August 14, the Japanese informed the Allied powers that they now agreed, without reservation, to a formal surrender and a cessation of all hostilities, to commence on August 15, the next day.

While this exchange was going on, we in northern Japan followed each development through our nightly news broadcast and prayed the Emperor could overrule his generals, who were determined to fight on, and bring the war to an end.

On August 15, our radio informed us that the Emperor was to broadcast by radio to the nation, informing the people of Japan's surrender and ordering them to lay down their arms. By the Emperor's order, Allied prisoners were not to be harmed.

The 15th of August dawned bright, warm, and clear in Japan. There was no sign from the Japanese guards that any momentous event was unfolding. As usual, the work party for the mine was paraded and counted. At 7:30 a.m. sharp, we began to march through the camp gate with our guards, on our mile-and-a-half journey to the mine.

At the mine it appeared to be another typical day, as Japanese mine workers and prisoners alike picked up their tools and went to their work stations to begin their tasks for the day. At 11:00 a.m., the sergeant of the guard, who had escorted us to the mine, sent for me. "*Hancho*," he said, "assemble all your men in stope number ten immediately." I looked at him with a surprised look and asked why. He snarled, "Do as you are told." In a few minutes we were all assembled in the dark, in an isolated, unused section of the mine. An explosive charge detonated here, if that is what they intended, would bring down the unstable roof, with tons of rock to be our tomb for eternity. What could I do? I expected something momentous was happening on the surface. I prayed that negotiations had not broken down, that the Emperor would carry out his radio announcement and his promise of surrender, and that his people would obey. But why herd us into this tomb-like, unused stope? Was it a trap? Would they push the plunger and bury us here forever, without a trace?

At 1:00 p.m., the sergeant of the guard came down to our location and said, "*Hancho*, tell your men we are going back to camp — no more work today." What a relief! When we had returned to the surface and were collecting our things, the Japanese foreman of the machine shop whispered to me that the Emperor had just spoken on the radio to tell the people of Japan the war was over. He winked at me and said in English, with a little smile, "*Hancho*, you go Canada now." Now we knew why we had been sequestered from the rest of the mine's workers. We were not to be allowed to hear the Emperor's voice or his message. We warily formed up and marched back to camp.

We knew the war was over and the Emperor had so informed the people of Japan. But what about the military? Would they obey the Emperor or would they revolt and carry on the war? Some of them did revolt, but their attempt to silence the Emperor failed and the leaders of the revolt were arrested. We were very vulnerable and completely defenceless in a dangerous power vacuum.

When we got back to the camp, we were counted. The camp commander took the salute, the guard was dismissed, and then, without a sign, the camp commander dismissed the work party to their barracks. What to do now? We had expected the camp commander to announce the cessation of hostilities and the surrender of Japan. But he didn't! As usual, his face was inscrutable. He turned on his heel and stalked off to his quarters. What was he thinking? What was he plotting? Why was he not facing his country's defeat and his emperor's announcement? Was his silence evidence he was not going to obey his orders from Tokyo?

In the meantime, as we pondered these questions, we decided we had to tell our men what had happened, as they were demanding to know why we had been sent back from the mine. We also told them that, while we may appear to be free, we were now in even more danger than before. We could not predict what would happen if the Japanese army decided to disobey the Emperor, and we did not wish to provoke an incident. Unfortunately, in the south of Japan after the armistice, some Japanese soldiers disobeyed the Emperor's orders after the surrender announcement and executed American prisoners. So we ate our rice, attended roll call, and went to bed as usual. I slept little that night.

The next morning, August 16, we paraded for work detail as usual at 7:15 a.m. At 7:30, after the count and other formalities, the camp commander declared, "*Kiowa yasumai, Kaisang,*" (Today is a holiday. Dismissed.) No announcement. No sign of a change.

The American captain, RSM Shore, and I had a conference. What to do? We were legally free perhaps, but surrounded by a volatile Japanese military seething with shame and resentment at their nation's dishonour. Many senior Japanese military officers committed seppuku, or ritual suicide, using their swords in the ancient manner. We were few in number, in very bad shape, and unarmed. We could not contact the occupation forces, nor they us. We decided that we would be safer sitting quietly for a while within the camp, while we hoped tempers would cool and the Allied armies would begin landing in Japan.

On August 17, the same thing happened. Work detail paraded, count made, military courtesies exchanged, the day declared a holiday by the camp commander. No announcement. Things were still calm outside and inside the fence. This day, we decided to face the camp commander and assert our authority and our new status as members of the occupying power. Why was he silent on the surrender? Maybe he knew something we didn't. Maybe he wasn't going to surrender! It seemed better to assume the initiative. Maybe he didn't know what to do. Perhaps he had no specific orders from his superiors. Japanese soldiers had deep respect for authority, so perhaps we should be authoritative. It was worth a try.

We met with the camp commander and told him we knew the war was over. He replied that it was *not* over, and how did we know the war was over anyway? So we took him into the barracks and showed him the radio, now tuned to the American armed forces radio station set up in Tokyo. The camp commander was dumbfounded. He suddenly realized that we had known what was going on for weeks and that he had not. We told him that now *we* were in command at Ohasi. From now on, we instructed, he would take his orders directly from the American captain, who was the senior Allied officer and now also the commander of the local Japanese prefecture. General MacArthur was now the supreme commander and governor of Japan — not the Emperor — and as MacArthur's soldiers, our orders would come from him, and then his orders would come from us. "What do you want?" he asked. We ordered him to dismiss the regular military guard and replace them with the Kempitai (the feared military police). He obeyed and we ordered him to remain in the camp with us.

After this meeting, we called our men together and told them they were no longer PoWs, but they were now soldiers of the occupying power. No one was to leave the camp and no contact under any circumstances was to be made with any Japanese without permission. The men had only one immediate question: "When do we barbecue the camp commander's pigs?" The answer: "Right now!" And so we had pork for supper.

After about a week of quiet, with a Kempitai corporal on guard at the main gate and no sign of the Japanese army, we decided we had to quickly improve our food ration for our sick and especially increase the amount of protein in our diet. We sent out into the countryside teams of 10 men, under an NCO, to carefully and quietly barter with the peasants for food: pork, eggs, vegetables, soya sauce, beans — anything we could buy. In exchange for fresh food, we traded army boots, tinned army rations, soap, and other military supplies that we took from the camp's military stores. This was extremely risky, but we found the civilians cautious but willing to trade, and very glad the war was over. This was a very dangerous action on our part but our starving men had to be fed immediately — the risk had to be taken. There were no incidents and the Japanese army did not intervene.

Now feeling somewhat bolder, we wanted to contact the occupying army that was slowly spreading its influence across Japan. The radio informed us that to locate us, a massive grid search of Japan would begin immediately from the air, with search planes launched from aircraft carriers at sea. We immediately painted the acronym PoW in white eight-foot letters on the roof of our biggest hut. Several days passed and then, on the 1st of September at 10:00 a.m., we heard a fighter plane coming in low from the ocean. Sure enough, there it was, a blue navy fighter with the white stars of the U.S. Navy on its wings, glinting in the sun. Oh God! Would he see us? Would he see our "PoW" on the roof? He passed a mile or so west of us and continued on out of sight, beyond a nearby mountain. He had failed to see us! But no, suddenly his cruising engine changed its pitch and we heard the familiar whining roar of a fighter plane in a dive. Around the mountain he came, down the centre of the valley where the camp lay and, with his big engine bellowing wide open, he flew over the flagpole at an altitude of one hundred feet, going four hundred miles an hour. Oh God, what a moment! Maybe, just maybe, we were going to get out of here after all — and alive!

We stood transfixed in the camp square, staring up at the blue messenger of hope from the sea. He climbed straight up on his tail for altitude, and at about five thousand feet he throttled back and circled high above us as we watched him send his radio message to his ship, "I've found a PoW camp!" Around the mountain he went and down the valley he came again, now with flaps down, wheels down, with air speed as slow as he dared. His canopy was back and we could see him clearly as he threw out a silver-coloured tin box with a long white streamer attached. It fluttered to the ground in the middle of the camp square. When we opened it, there was a handwritten note on a card that said, "Lieutenant Claude E. Newton, from the *John Hancock*, 50 miles offshore. Have radioed location. Put out markers." In the tin box were several fluorescent-covered strips of cloth and instructions that said: "If you need food, arrange the strips to read F; if you need medicine, arrange the strips to read M; if you need a combat paratroop drop, arrange the strips to read P." We arranged the strips to read F and M. Again, for the third time, he went around the mountain and came down the valley, and as he passed over us at about two hundred feet, he waggled his wings, opened the throttle of his mighty engine, and headed straight out to sea.

The camp went wild. They had found us and they were prepared to save us by armed intervention if needed. I will never forget the joy and relief of that September morning as long as I live. Our lives of humiliation and slavery were over. We were now reunited with a victorious army that had overcome its enemy. We were not forgotten. They hadn't written us off. They were going to rescue us! These and a thousand other thoughts flashed through our minds, as slowly but surely the

Liberation Day — September 15, 1945.

idea took hold that this may be the turning point towards life, freedom, and family, and away from captivity, fear, anxiety, and miserable death on this godforsaken mountainous island! But what next? How would they respond to our discovery? What would they do now?

At about 2:30 in the afternoon, we found out. The quiet of the valley was disturbed by, at first, a slight murmur from the sea, then a distant rumble, and then a full-throated, earth-shattering roar as 14 big carrier torpedo bombers appeared at five thousand feet in formation above the camp, led by our little blue fighter with the white stars of the U.S. on its wings. After one low pass over the camp in formation, they formed up, line astern, went behind the mountain, and came down the valley at two hundred miles per hour, one at a time. As each reached the camp perimeter, it dropped its load of supplies with attached white parachutes. The chutes caught easily and drifted down to earth within the camp, bearing their precious loads of F and M. They made two complete passes, leaving behind over eight thousand pounds of food and medicine. One of the big bundles broke away from its chute and crashed through the camp commander's office, wrecking it.

After dropping the supplies, the young pilots of these 15 airplanes put on an air show for us and the awestruck Japanese. I have never seen such stunt flying in such big planes in my life, as each tried to outdo the other. Then, suddenly the show was over. The planes disappeared, line astern, behind the mountain, then down the valley one at a time at three hundred feet, engines wide open and wings waggling as they headed south for their floating home at sea. It was an awe-inspiring show of raw military power and it left us and its Japanese audience suitably impressed. Those navy fliers left no doubt in anybody's mind that this little pocket of Allied prisoners at Ohasi was very, very important to them.

In one of the bundles of medicine dropped there was a substance called penicillin, with detailed instructions on its use. Our doctor had never heard of it and was astonished at the results as he began to use it on his worst cases.

Senior officer and NCOs at Ohasi.

That night, we had a feast that lasted for hours. The shock of the calories nearly killed us! With the food and the miracle drug, the doctor began to see his patients respond with amazing speed.

The next day, a fighter plane flew over and dropped a note that said, "Goodbye from crew of *Hancock*, big friends come tomorrow." At about 10:00 a.m., three gigantic B29 bombers appeared. They circled the camp, flew up-wind a couple of miles, and began their run at a very low altitude. We saw their giant bomb-bay doors open and suddenly a wooden platform — upon which was loaded 30 60-gallon oil drums — was dropped. To each oil drum was attached a coloured nylon chute, and each was packed with tinned rations and supplies of every kind. Soon the air was filled with 90 60-gallon oil drums, swinging leisurely beneath their chutes, coming to earth over an area of a square mile or so. In one pass they dropped 18,000 pounds of food and supplies of all kinds. In the eyes of the nearby Japanese villagers, we had now gone from starvation and poverty to wealth beyond measure. Being North Americans, it occurred to us that, since our newfound wealth was scattered all over hell's half acre, we should have the Japanese civilians find and bring our oil drums to the camp, which they were glad to do if we let them keep the nylon chutes and some of the food as payment.

That night, we had another big party, only now everyone was dressed in a new uniform of his choice: navy, army, marine. The next morning, promptly at the same time, three lumbering six-engined giants from the Marianas made their run and again deposited another three tons of supplies on Ohasi. Again the industrious Japanese, with much bowing and hissing, dutifully delivered the aerial bounty to their conquerors. By now the camp was beginning to look like an oil refinery, with over 150 60-gallon oil drums stacked on the square.

The next morning, the same thing. Right on schedule, and this time with red and green rockets being fired as salutes we guessed, the Marianas milk run dropped its supplies on target.

The next day dawned bright and clear, but with a high wind blowing from the sea. The bombers appeared on time, but this time when they dropped, some of the parachute lines were snapped in the high winds and the oil drums fell straight down as deadly missiles. Several hit the camp, crashed through the roofs of the huts, smashed against the concrete floors of the huts, and exploded. One such drum was packed with canned peaches, and I can assure you that no surface avoided being smeared with peach mist anywhere in that hut. There were several near-misses of ours and Japanese personnel, and several Japanese houses in the nearby village were badly damaged. The next day the same thing happened and as I was fleeing from the camp to a nearby railroad tunnel, I looked up to see that I was right under a cloud of falling 60-gallon oil drums now free from their parachutes. It was a terrifying moment. Was I to be killed after all? Not by a hated enemy, but by the clumsy kindness of my well-meaning American friends?

Again the camp was hit by drums full of such things as cans of cooked sausages and baked beans. Something had to be done. We now had tons of food and supplies and more were arriving at the rate of nine tons a day. Besides, it was getting to be very dangerous and the camp had begun to look as if it had been shelled by artillery. So we painted two words on the roof: NO MORE! The next day, the big birds came from the Marianas, and as we watched with bated breath from the safety of the nearby railroad tunnel, they circled the camp and, without opening their bomb-bay doors, flew back out to sea, never to be seen again. It was great fun while it lasted, but it was getting to be too much of a good thing.

The immediate, organized action to drop so much food, clothing, and medicine into the camp was typical of the Americans. When you consider the cost of the delivery system and the amount of aid they provided and the speed with which they delivered it, you can only wonder. This generous and timely response to our needs saved many lives and it says a great deal about the values of those American sailors and flyers and about the mighty, civilized nation that stood behind them. No Canadian, as he gazed in wonder at our American ally's rescue efforts, will ever forget their concern for us and their generosity.

Now we settled down to caring for our many sick and to some serious eating. About the 10th of September, a Canadian Army captain, escorted by a corporal, walked calmly into our camp. He was from Canadian headquarters in Tokyo, and he told us that the Americans had informed him of the location of the camp but of course did not know the nationalities of its occupants, so he and his corporal came by train to see what they could find. He told us that our former captors in Hong Kong had been arrested and were being held on various charges, including murder. Colonel Tokunaga, the Hong Kong camp commander, was among those on trial for the murder of Canadian prisoners, and so was the "Kamloops Kid."

At about this time, I decided to go back to the mine with some of my men to say goodbye to the Japanese civilians who had befriended us and who had often tried to be helpful. I especially wanted to say goodbye to the fatherly old foreman of the machine shop, who had been kind to me on a personal basis. It was both a joyous and sad meeting. We were all happy that the war was over and we Canadians could go home, and yet we were sad at the knowledge that this would be our last "sayonara." I promised my old Japanese foreman friend that I would take his advice and return to school as soon as I got home.

"*Hancho*, you go Canada now." These words, whispered on August 15, the day the Emperor spoke, will never be forgotten, nor will the goodwill of the old man who spoke them. I developed no hatred for the people of Japan. Most of them were as kind to us as they could be under the harsh rules of their military dictatorship. The Japanese lost 2,700,000 servicemen and civilians during the war. Millions more were left starving, homeless, and wounded. The common people of Japan and their loyal soldiers were unwitting cannon fodder for their cruel and evil rulers, who forced them to act out their crazy dreams of the military conquest of East Asia. As usual, it was the common people of Japan who paid the terrible price for the military imperialism of their ruling elite.

We also visited the camp graveyard and sadly said one last goodbye to our comrades who had found their last resting place so far from home. It seemed to me an unjust reward for such brave young men. Great tears I could not control welled up in my eyes and streamed down my cheeks as I gazed down at them for the last time.

On September 14, a naval airplane flew in from the sea and dropped a note to inform us that an American naval task force would enter Kamaishi Harbour to evacuate all prisoners on the following day.

September 15 was a beautiful, clear, warm fall day in Japan. Early in the morning, an American fleet appeared and anchored in Kamaishi Harbour. Large tank-landing craft beached themselves and in haste disgorged a force of marines and their armoured vehicles. Soon, a motorized column of marines arrived at the Ohasi camp. They were led by a marine colonel and they were armed to the teeth. These were veterans of the long Pacific campaign. They had survived many terrible encounters with the Japanese in their march across the Pacific and they looked the part. I never saw a more comforting sight. After our captain saluted the colonel, they embraced. The colonel then told us how he planned to evacuate us and gave specific orders as to how this was to be done. After he issued his orders, he asked, "Are there any questions?" Our captain said, "Yes, I have one. What in the hell took you so long to get here?" That brought a smile to those tough, weather-beaten faces.

We were already packed and ready, and after our sick were loaded, the order was given to "mount up" and we headed for the harbour, with the marines warily manning their .50 calibre machine guns. But before I left, I removed the camp commander's sword from his sword belt and stuck it in mine. I also took one of the guard's rifles for good measure and said "sayonara" to Ohasi forever.

During the period from August 15 until September 15, the day of Japan's surrender until the day of our rescue, no sign was ever seen of the Japanese army that was encamped in our area. Thank heaven! With some exceptions across Japan, they simply obeyed their Emperor's command to lay down their arms and return to their homes.

When we pulled into the harbour area in the bright sunshine, there, riding at anchor under the Stars and Stripes, was a large armada of naval ships: a cruiser, destroyers, minesweepers, and several large tank-landing craft, beached with their bows open to receive their landed armoured vehicles, and a swarm of wary

Canadian PoW forced to work in Japan.

marines in their camouflage greens. In the centre of this grey, menacing fleet was a big white American hospital ship, the *Mercy*. I will never forget that wonderful sight.

In minutes, we were ferried to the *Mercy*, where we were welcomed by the captain, who shook each of us by hand as we came aboard. In moments we were stripped and our brand-new uniforms — including socks, shoes, and underwear — were thrown over the side into the harbour. Next, we filed naked into the ship, where a gang of sailors in bathing suits sprayed us with DDT and scrubbed us with navy soap in hot showers, until we glowed. The very sick and stretcher cases disappeared and were immediately put to bed in the ship's hospital. Next, we were outfitted from head to toe in brand-new naval uniforms, according to our rank. Then we were each inspected carefully by a team of doctors who immediately ordered treatment for leg ulcers and other matters that did not require immediate hospitalization. We were then asked if we wished to bring charges against any of the Japanese officers ashore. We declined. We were given a message form and told we could send any message to anyone anywhere in the world and that these messages had top priority over other wireless traffic. Our families, 12,000 miles away, were informed of our rescue within a matter of hours.

Now it was time for lunch in the ship's cafeteria: soup, milk, and freshly baked bread with butter. After lunch, we were shown to our comfortable sleeping quarters. At this point, a petty officer told me I was wanted on the bridge. On the bridge, in my brand-new lieutenant's naval uniform, I was informed by the captain that I was to be transferred to the cruiser as the admiral's guest. A launch pulled alongside within minutes and we sailed off across the harbour to the cruiser. As I climbed the gangway to the deck, pipes twittered and I was met by the officer of the deck and his attendants. I was taken straight to the cruiser's sick bay, where I was examined again by a doctor. The doctor told me I was invited to dinner with the admiral and the ship's officers, in the ward room at 7:00 p.m., and in the meantime I was to be shown my quarters for a rest. I was escorted to a gleaming, spotless cabin by two Filipino mess attendants who turned down the white sheets of my bunk and said they would be back for me at 6:45 p.m. As I lay back on my bunk and closed my eyes in the darkened cabin, I heard the anchor chain of the mighty warship rattling up into its locker. Soon I began to feel the gentle rocking motion of the cruiser as she gathered speed and knifed her way out into the open ocean, at the head of the task force bound for Tokyo.

That night, I was the guest of honour in the ward room, sitting at the right hand of the admiral. When I entered the room, the ship's officers all rose and the admiral introduced me to each of them in turn.

For dinner, on a spotless white tablecloth with gleaming silver, white-coated stewards served us chicken, ice cream, and coffee. After dinner, they insisted I tell them how we Canadians managed to be in Japan and how we had survived our imprisonment. They listened in amazement and with great interest, and after an hour or so I was escorted back to my cabin for the night. As I closed my eyes to prepare for sleep after this exhausting day, I began to realize it was not a dream. Our prayers had been answered. My men were safe, we had finally escaped, and we were now in the hands of our generous and capable friends, on the first leg of our journey home. The shooting war was over.

We had made it! We were free at last! As I lay quietly on my bunk in the darkened cabin, listening to the faint hum of the big cruiser's turbines and enjoying the gentle rocking motion of the open sea, I wondered at the cost. How many of my comrades had been so lucky? I didn't know it then, but very soon I was to learn to my sorrow that 557 of these young men would remain behind on alien soil, to sleep forever where they had fallen as casualties of battle, cruelty, or starvation. Unlike us, they would never see their homes and their loved ones or hear their mothers' voices again. As for the regiment, it never laid down its arms until ordered to do so, and, to a man, the Royal Rifles never quit during the battle on the island or in those ghastly prison camps. Even to this day, they remain bloody but unbowed — their spirit will live forever. I will never forget them.

Chapter Eight

Going Home

On the 17th of September, we arrived in Tokyo Harbour. In the harbour was an awesome spectacle. Hundreds upon hundreds of warships were anchored, row on row, as far as the eye could see, with their Stars and Stripes and pendants fluttering in the breeze. Here, assembled in one place, was the mighty American fleet, as well as the warships of Great Britain, Australia, Canada, and other nations. There were aircraft carriers, battleships, cruisers, destroyers, transports, minesweepers, tankers, submarines, and countless other types of naval vessels. This was the largest assembly of naval power in one place in the history of the world, and a sight that would be never seen again.

By this time, within its giant wartime navy, the United States had one hundred aircraft carriers at sea. Almost all of these were riding at anchor, side by side, across a seemingly endless expanse of open harbour as far as the eye could see. As these great rows of giant flat-tops swung at their moorings, there was a constant traffic of fleet aircraft landing and taking off from the decks of these stationary giants, like busy worker bees at a beehive. The roar of their engines never ceased from dawn to dusk. The harbour was a constant scene of action as grey-painted ships of every kind and size busily came and went about their various missions within the fleet. I could not help but wonder what the Japanese, who had awakened this sleeping American giant with their attack on Pearl Harbor just somewhat less than four years ago, were thinking now. Who of them could have dreamed of the consequences of that cowardly attack?

August 1945 — Shamshuipo PoW camp.

Those of us who were not hospitalized on the *Mercy* were transferred to an APA, the USNS *Hyde*, anchored in the bay. (An APA is a naval vessel used to transport marines to an enemy shore.) We said thank you and goodbye to our rescuers and were soon aboard our new floating home.

The *Hyde* was a specialized naval vessel designed to house, transport, and land marines on a hostile shore. She was like a floating hotel with comfortable quarters, a large hospital, and all the amenities required for a very large landing force. From the stern of the *Hyde*, we could see our former place of employment, the Nippon Kokan shipyard, where we had worked for so long. Beyond that, Mount Fuji rose majestically to survey the harbour, packed with the ships of the conquerors of Japan.

Within a few days, the *Hyde* weighed anchor and steamed out to sea, headed for the island of Guam. After a pleasant journey of a few days, we arrived at Guam, which American forces had taken from the Japanese about a year earlier. Japanese stragglers were still free in the jungle. The island was one of the main staging bases that was to have been used for the American assault on Japan.

Guam had hospital facilities for more than 500,000 Allied wounded and had hundreds of newly built hospitals fully staffed with doctors, nurses, and support personnel. We were taken to the 103rd Fleet Hospital. It was an immense Quonset building that, while staffed with a full complement of doctors and nurses, had never yet seen a single patient. Since the planned American invasion of Japan had been made unnecessary by the Japanese surrender, we were its first and only patients.

When the staff of the hospital found out we were rescued PoWs, and from Canada, the generosity and hospitality natural to Americans rose to new heights to ensure we were treated like royalty. We were carefully examined, put on special diets, and given another new uniform. We had movies every night and, as a special treat, were allowed one bottle of beer each day. All dental work was immediately undertaken and everything imaginable was done to help us regain our health.

As the senior Canadian, I was responsible for 68 survivors of nearly four years of imprisonment. It was my job to see they got home safely, and each day I had to report their presence and status to the head of the hospital. Otherwise, I was free to roam the island, visit other PoW groups from other countries who were on

August 1945 — Argyle Street PoW camp.

their way home, and observe the many Marine combat units that had been assembled on Guam for the invasion of Japan.

One day, some American military police came to the hospital to see me. For some reason, their interpreter was absent and they wanted me to go to a small camp where some Japanese were being held as prisoners of war. These men had been captured alive because they were unconscious or so badly wounded that they had not died fighting. Since then, every precaution was taken by their American guards to keep them alive and to dissuade them from committing suicide. They wanted me to interpret their wishes to these Japanese prisoners. There had been an earlier misunderstanding and the Americans wanted to reassure their prisoners that they meant them no harm or dishonour. This was easily accomplished, even with my limited Japanese. These poor souls faced disgrace and an uncertain future when they were forced to return to their homes in Japan.

Any and every request was granted immediately and our convalescence progressed rapidly. We gained an average of a pound a day and soon all signs of malnutrition — such as boils, pellagra, and skin ulcers — disappeared under the watchful eyes of the American naval doctors. After several weeks, our doctors told me they believed we were well enough to undertake the sea voyage from Guam to the United States. I agreed and we were given top priority status for the voyage home. Three days later, we said goodbye again and boarded another APA, the USNS *Catron*.

The *Catron* was bound for San Francisco, with a stop in Hawaii. Our fellow passengers on the *Catron* were the first American combat troops to return home from the Pacific theatre. They were the first of the hundreds of thousands who would be returning from the Pacific. Because of their long service, many decorations for bravery, and the number of battles they had fought in, they were given priority status as the first men to return to the U.S. So many points were allocated for the above-mentioned factors and these men were the highest point-holders and thus given the first shipping space available.

They were a fascinating, bemedalled bunch from every service, mostly marines. They were also the tough veterans of many bloody, protracted battles of extermination with the Japanese at Truck, Tarawa, Quajeilin, Okinawa, Saipan, and Iwo Jima, just to mention a few. Most of them could hardly believe they had survived the awful, no-quarter-given conflict of the past four years, and they were delighted to be going home to their families.

Again we were given special status on the ship and were allocated the best sleeping quarters and messing arrangements on board.

After approximately two weeks at sea, the *Catron* docked off Angel Island in San Francisco Bay. The next morning at nine o'clock, she was warped over to a large dock that held a huge welcoming crowd of civilians and a marine band. The gangplank was lowered and all was made ready to debark.

The captain and his officers were drawn up on the quarter-deck and the Canadians were paraded before them, with me at their head. The ship fell silent and the captain gave a short speech. He said, "The Canadian Army will have the honour to go ashore first. The armed forces of the United States are proud to be able to be of some assistance to their Canadian allies, who have fought so bravely at Hong Kong and who have suffered so much for an Allied victory." He said he spoke for all those present when he wished us good luck and a safe and speedy return to our homes. I then gave a short speech in reply and said that we were grateful for their timely rescue, their transport home, and their kind and generous treatment. At this point we saluted and I shook hands with the captain.

The entry chain to the gangplank was dropped, and one by one my men — with their kit bags, Japanese swords, rifles, Japanese flags, and other trophies of war — filed down the gangplank. The band began to play and the entire ship's company and all of the veteran passengers lined the rail, every porthole, and other ship's openings to wave goodbye.

Suddenly, halfway down the gangplank, one of our men stopped, put down his kit bag, out of which protruded a large Japanese flag, and turned his face up to the packed crowd of watchers on the ships towering above him. I was still at the top of the gangplank and I motioned to him to get moving and to stop blocking our progress. When it became obvious that he wanted to speak, the band stopped playing, the crowd fell silent, and those on the ship stared down at him with close attention. He then spoke in a loud voice: "If you Yanks have any more trouble with the Japanese, you know where to find us!" With that, he turned and proceeded down the gangway.

There was a stunned silence, and as the humour of this audacity struck home, the waiting passengers on the ship let out a mighty guffaw at such totally unexpected effrontery. They howled with glee at these remarks, and, suddenly, to commend his sally, a blizzard of various kinds of headgear came sailing through the air, flung by our delighted audience to speed us on our way and to show their approval for the gutsy little guy from Quebec.

We went straight from the docks to a waiting train bound for Seattle. At Seattle, we spent the night in a U.S. Army barracks and were allowed to go into the city until 11:00 p.m. While in the city, I called the mother of the pilot who had discovered our camp at Ohasi, Lieutenant Claude Newton. I identified myself and asked if he was home. She said no, he would not be home until the *Hancock* returned from Japan in another six weeks, but he was alive and had survived his tour of duty. She said she would be sure to tell him I called. I later wrote him and sent him a group picture of the men of Ohasi, whom he was instrumental in rescuing.

In the morning, we took the ferry to Victoria, and from there we went to a military hospital at Gordon Head, where I turned over my 68 men to the commanding officer. After 49 months, I was not only free, but also on Canadian soil at last!

At the Gordon Head PoW centre, we were again carefully examined and issued with brand-new Canadian uniforms. A group of local women came into the centre and hand-tailored our new uniforms and sewed on our new Hong Kong shoulder flashes and badges of rank. We were visited by the mayor of Victoria and the famous General Worthington. Our beds were piled with letters from home, and we all used the telephone to make our first voice contact with our loved ones. When leave was granted to go into the city of Victoria, we found we were celebrities. Everyone, it seemed, wanted to shake our hands and welcome us home. Merchants refused payment for our purchases and all meals in the local restaurants were free to those who wore the Hong Kong shoulder patch.

Finally, the doctors and the centre commander agreed we were fit to travel. Orders were cut, our kit bags were packed, and we headed for home with first-class sleeping and dining-car tickets on the Canadian Pacific Railway. It seemed that my promise to my men, made earlier in September in Ohasi that they would be home for Christmas, was about to come true.

At each major city, as the train travelled east, there was a reception committee to greet us when we stopped and to shower us with gifts of fruit, homemade cookies, and letters of appreciation from the city fathers.

Free at last — Victoria, B.C., 1945.

I arrived at Union Station in Toronto a week before Christmas, to be met by my aunt and uncle and my cousins, who came to take me home. Before we left the station, my comrades who were going on to Quebec and the Maritimes filed out of the train and, in the middle of the station, gave the "quair fella" from Ontario three rousing cheers in farewell. Once more the tears flowed as I said goodbye and shook hands and embraced each and every one of those wonderful young men who had kept faith with me on the green-clad battlefield of Hong Kong and in the grim prison camps of Japan. What wonderful, brave comrades they were and have remained to this day.

I felt no bitterness towards those who ordered me to Hong Kong. While I know their real motives were never revealed and their later Royal Commission of Inquiry was a deliberate white-wash, I accepted with no rancour their decision to send us to Hong Kong simply as a blunder that often happens in war.

What was significant to me, however, was how my comrades, the young soldiers of the Royal Rifles, reacted when they were plunged into the military crisis of December 8, 1941. When the Japanese attacked, we had no interest in fixing blame for our predicament and no thought of second-guessing our leaders. Despite the odds, and without hesitation, we did our utmost to repel the invasion of the island. We did our best to slow down the Japanese timetable of conquest and inflicted upon them the greatest punishment we could. Though bottled up on Stanley Peninsula in a hopeless position and running out of ammunition, food, and water, until the garrison surrendered we remained defiant.

When the governor surrendered the island to the Japanese, those of us who were still standing refused to surrender until 8:30 p.m. on Christmas Day, when we were given written orders to do so, signed by the governor himself. We were on the losing side in the Battle of Hong Kong, but not through lack of courage or determination to uphold the honour of our country.

After my Christmas leave was over, I reported back to Wolseley Barracks, where I had begun my soldier's life six and a half years before. From Wolseley, I was immediately transferred to Westminster Military Hospital in London. Here I began my convalescence and started to recover my health. I was allowed passes to go into the city and the occasional pass to go to my uncle's home in Stratford for the weekend. In Stratford I was treated like a celebrity and spoke before the Lion's Club, the chamber of commerce, and other community groups.

As the weeks passed, I began to face a real dilemma. My whole life, since I was 17, had been spent in the army. The army was not only my vocation, it was my family. Not only that, I loved the military service and, with my aptitude as a leader, I knew I could succeed in a military career. On the other hand, I desperately wanted a family of my own. I knew, however, that because soldiers often lived in isolated camps, a family and a military career was a poor combination. I also knew that in peacetime a military career could be both frustrating and not very challenging. At the same time, I was very apprehensive of my fate in the civilian world, as I had only a Grade 10 high-school diploma. I was afraid to give up the army, where I was secure and appreciated, for the uncertainty and the risk of the world outside. At last, full of conflict, I decided to accept the uncertainty of a civilian life and return to school to prepare myself for a career outside the army. And so, after three months in London, one beautiful day at the end of March 1946, I was discharged from the hospital and the army after nearly seven years of service. I said goodbye to my fellow patients, shook hands with the doctors and the nurses with a mighty lump in my throat, and, dressed in a brand-new uniform adorned with my red Hong Kong shoulder flashes and my medal ribbons, walked down the driveway for the last time to my waiting car.

I went straight to the railway station and took the train to my uncle's home in Stratford. As the train sped across the beautiful green farmlands of Ontario and as I watched this bountiful, peaceful landscape unfold through the windows of the train, I realized how fortunate we Canadians were and how lucky I was to be a citizen in this, the best country in the world. As I sat alone in the almost empty railway day coach, I thought about my fallen comrades and the past. I realized how lucky I had been and I was thankful to have been spared. I promised myself that I would make good use of the life that now stretched before me. Having seen a slice of life in the Far East, I would never again take my priceless Canadian citizenship for granted, and never would I cease to be proud to be a Canadian.

On that day in March, this soldier's story ended. The war was finally over. The soldiers of Canada's victorious army had gone back to their families and to their civilian callings. The bustling military camps were closed and silent. The parade squares were empty and no longer reverberated to the sergeants' commands and the rhythmic ring of marching feet. The uniform I so proudly wore must now be replaced by a civilian suit. No longer at dawn would I be awakened by reveille or hear in the evening the bugler sound the last post. After nearly seven years, it was time to say goodbye. Except for the memories, all that was past. Now I had to go back to school, get an education, and find a place for myself in the big, free, and exciting world outside the army. I thought if I worked hard and was lucky, perhaps I could find somebody to help me form another family — my own.

Chapter Nine

Back to School

In the spring of 1945, as the war neared its end and an Allied victory seemed assured, the Parliament of Canada began to plan for the re-entry of nearly one million soldiers, sailors, and airmen into Canada's civilian life and its economy. One of the many federal government programs to help returning veterans adjust to civilian life was called the Veterans' Educational Rehabilitation Program, or "rehab scheme" for short. This scheme, in essence, was designed to assist qualified servicemen and -women to return to school to complete an education that had been disrupted by enlistment in Canada's armed forces. For example, if a serviceman upon enlistment had not completed his senior matriculation (five years in those days) and had only completed three years of high school, he could return to his studies and complete his senior matriculation. Then, if he had the service requirements as part of the rehab scheme, he could go on to university, and again, if he had the service requirements, he could attend and complete a university course of study. The rules were very clear and simple and made for amazing flexibility as long as you met the service requirements. The basic rehab rules and requirements were as follows:

1. Each serviceman or -woman was granted one tuition-free month of education for every month served in the armed forces in World War II; and

2. each qualified applicant was paid $60 per month as a living allowance during a successful month of attendance at an approved rehab educational institution.

Because Canada's high schools would be swamped by thousands of veterans who wanted to resume and finish their high-school courses, special "rehab schools" were established throughout the country, usually in now-empty army barracks. These schools were staffed by retired teachers and members of the armed forces who had returned to Canada and who had been professional teachers before the war.

Now, thousands of veterans still in their service uniforms — no civilian clothing was yet available — went back to rehab schools to finish their high-school education. Bomber pilots, tank crewmen, sailors, battery commanders, and soldiers by the thousands of Canada's army rubbed shoulders as they attended their various rehab high-school classes across the country. Thousands more entered Canada's universities. These grizzled warriors of Canada's victorious forces who had met and defeated in countless battles the Kriegsmarine, the Luftwaffe, and the Wehrmach, as well as the Imperial Forces of the Rising Sun, now sat as students in their military garb in crowded university classes with 18-year-old boys and girls who had just graduated from high school and left home for the first time.

Many of these veterans had served five or six years overseas in the thick of the fighting in every theatre of war. Forty-six thousand of their comrades had given their lives and were buried in military graveyards all over the world; a further 53,000 had been wounded. Now all these veterans wanted was to return to their homes and a normal life. They wanted jobs and above all they wanted a family. They had seen the world and its people and now they were in a hurry to make up for lost time. They had little sympathy for the idea that university was a place to help adolescents reach maturity. They had other priorities. The professors of the ivy-clad institutions were in for a shock. These veterans, some of whom had commanded a thousand men in battle, a bomber over Germany, or a warship at sea, were entirely different from the youths they had been teaching up to now. These veterans were not the passive, inexperienced, easily impressed high-school teenagers they had grown accustomed to. These guys possessed a brimming self-confidence in their view of the outside world that they had just returned from. They were aggressive, demanding, and, worst of all, they were sceptical. They were not overly impressed by caps and gowns and the other trappings of the university. On top of this, they had a thirst for knowledge, an urgency, and a motivation the poor professors had never before felt or seen. Woe betide the professor who came poorly prepared to class or was vague in his pronouncements. His veteran students who had done their homework would pounce on him like a hawk on a pigeon and the academic feathers would fly.

The really competent professors revelled in the challenge and the new atmosphere in the classroom posed by these "show me" veterans. They looked forward to each class and the give and take of the intellectual intercourse of motivated adults. University teaching took on a new and unexpected dimension as these veteran students, most of them in their late 20s, came to learn, but from their unusual experience they also had much to teach professors who had gained their knowledge from a book. They had little reluctance to tell professors some things about mankind and how people actually behave that sprang not from academic theory but from personal, practical, worldwide experience. These students had the temerity, when provoked, to stand up in the classroom and in a loud and confident voice tell the professor that he was *wrong*!

The veterans doubled and, in some cases, tripled the student body of Canada's universities. They changed our country forever and the face of higher education in Canada because now thousands of the sons and daughters of working-class families could go to university, get straight As, and graduate into a job or a profession that would not have been possible just a few years ago. Their military service to their country had made that possible. Rehab broke the mould and opened up higher education to the masses. And the masses seized the opportunity to enter the heretofore exclusive world of the educated. What an exciting time for the veteran and non-veteran students, the professors, the universities, and Canada.

The $60 living allowance mentioned earlier was entirely conditional not only upon attendance at rehab school or university but upon successfully passing periodic tests and quarterly exams. Usually, one exam or test failure meant you were out. Public money was not going to be spent on veterans whose attendance or exam results weren't acceptable — and it wasn't. However, few veterans were dropped from the program. By now they knew the value of education and no students before or since were so highly motivated to succeed as these.

I can think of no government expenditure in Canada's history that paid such handsome dividends to the nation as the rehab program, which opened the door of opportunity to so many who otherwise would never have been able to attend university and become doctors, lawyers, engineers, and business leaders of their communities. The program was successful; it lifted students, teachers, and educational institutions alike to new levels of importance and excellence.

The rules were simple, the bureaucracy minimal, and the students highly motivated. Above all, you had to perform or else you were out. There was no nonsense and no waste of taxpayers' money on slackers. This was simply a reward for those who qualified, with a big "if" — *if* you performed!

I learned about this wonderful education gift from my grateful country when I arrived at the Gordon Head PoW reception centre on Vancouver Island just outside the garden city of Victoria in October of 1945. Could I qualify? I was 23 years old with a Grade 10 "commercial" certificate which meant I needed to gain a full five-year senior matriculation in academic subjects before I could enter university. Therefore, I needed to start at the bottom or the first grade of high school and catch up on five years of academic subjects. My commercial certificate didn't count. I had accumulated 79 months of military service, which meant I could go to school with free tuition and $60 per month as a veteran student for nearly 10 full school years.

I discussed my situation with a rehab counsellor sent around to explain the scheme to us at Gordon Head who said the scheme had not contemplated enrolling students with fewer than two or three years or junior matriculation standing in academic subjects and he doubted that, at this late date, rehab would be able to provide assistance to one such as me, with so little education, regardless of my long service and my military record. My heart sank as I remembered promising myself and my old Japanese foreman before I left Ohasi in Japan that I would return to school. This at first glance appeared to be a promise that was going to be impossible to keep.

I spoke to our head doctor at Gordon Head and asked him if I could be discharged immediately so that I could return to school. He listened to my story and firmly and quietly said that from my medical records on the desk before him I was in no condition to even leave the hospital, let alone return to school. He said the army wouldn't hear of a discharge and that I'd be lucky to be allowed to go home to Ontario for a few days for Christmas. What a horrible feeling of disappointment. Now I began to realize the price I had paid for running away from home, quitting school, and rejecting my kindly Uncle George's wise advice to complete my education before joining the Army.

As I sat alone in my hospital room at Gordon Head, I was forced to take stock. I had a Grade 10 commercial certificate and just over three thousand dollars in back pay. My military experience and skills in a country weary of war and demobilizing as quickly as it could seemed to offer little opportunity or encouragement for me. My only hope was to gain an education to prepare me for life as a civilian, unless I wanted to stay in the army, which I loved and which was the easy course to follow.

As I mentioned earlier, I left Gordon Head to be home in Stratford for Christmas. After Christmas of 1945, I was immediately hospitalized at Westminster Military Hospital in London, Ontario. Here, as my eyesight and general health began to improve, I lobbied and plotted to gain my discharge from the hospital and the army. I needed to return to rehab school as soon as possible because the rehab program was coming to an end. The Royal Rifles had been among the first Canadian troops to be committed to battle, and because the survivors of the Battle of Hong Kong had been transferred to and imprisoned in Japan and Japan surrendered four months after Germany, we were the last to come home by nearly a year. As the demand for rehab high schools diminished, they began to close one by one while I was still in the hospital. It appeared time was not on my side. I had to get out of that hospital before it was too late. It seemed that no good deed would go unpunished. While I lobbied the chief medical officer of the hospital for a speedy discharge, I also pestered the rehab admittance office in downtown London for an admission to rehab school.

I soon found out that senior military medical officers are a breed unto themselves who brook no advice or interference from anyone and who do not take kindly to a mere soldier who tells them, first, that he is well when he isn't, and second, that he shouldn't be in hospital in the first place when the doctors say he should be. In fact, I found out senior medical officers can become downright nasty to anyone telling them, or even suggesting to them, what to do on army medical matters, and that includes generals! I didn't reach the point of insubordination but to the medical commander of Westminster Hospital I became more than a mild irritant. I was told that if I persisted in pestering the authorities about a discharge much more, I would be in real danger of being clapped in irons.

From the rehab bureaucrats downtown, I received one blunt no after another. There was no give with these guys. Their reasons were simple; the only openings they had were for veterans who had completed three years of high school before enlistment. No, my Grade 10 commercial certificate was of no help and could not be counted.

It seemed to me that, as one of the longest serving soldiers in World War II in the Canadian army, I should be given a little special consideration. But no! As far as they were concerned, the case was closed, the sentence handed down, and that was that! "Besides," they said, "they won't even let you out of the damn hospital."

Finally, against his misgivings, the chief medical officer of Westminster granted me a discharge from the hospital to become effective March 27, 1946. As soon as I learned of this, I phoned the rehab admissions office and said I wanted to see Captain Burke, who was the chief administrative officer of that office. His secretary asked me to state my reasons for an interview. I told her what they were, and after a long pause she came back to the phone and told me the interview was denied. My case had been reviewed and there was no point in any further discussion.

The next day, I asked for a day pass from the hospital, and when it was granted, I got dressed up in my new uniform, adorned with my Hong Kong shoulder flashes, my sergeant major's crowns, my seven-year service chevrons, my wound stripe, my service medals, my MID ("Mentioned in Dispatch") oak leaf commendation, and my shiny black Royal Rifles cap badge on its red back-drop. Thus dressed up like a military Christmas tree going to a parade but without a brass band and the Canadian army battle flag flying before me, I marched into Captain Burke's office in downtown London at precisely 9:00 a.m. The captain's secretary looked at me, no doubt wondering if World War III had commenced, and warily asked me what I wanted.

I said, "I want to see Captain Burke."

She said in reply, "I'm sorry, but Captain Burke is not in."

That was a mistake, because I said, "Fine, I'll wait."

I then sat down in a nearby chair and stared straight ahead, like a smouldering volcano that might erupt at any moment. I sometimes wonder what I would have done if one of Captain Burke's staff superior in rank to me had ordered me to leave the office and return to the hospital. Since I would never disobey an order, I would have had to obey. But such an order never came.

Finally, at 11:30 Captain Burke gave in and I was asked into his office to take a seat placed in front of his desk. He coldly and correctly informed me of the facts, which we both knew I fully understood. He said he was very sorry but he could do nothing to help me. When he was finished, I pushed back my chair and stood up and looked into his eyes.

"Captain," I said, "the Parliament of Canada has passed a law that guarantees me 79 months of education as a reward for my service to my country. I was one of those Canadians who were first committed to battle and the last to come home. I and my regiment served with distinction against overwhelming enemy forces in an impossible military situation, and I never laid down my arms or quit my post until I was ordered to do so in writing by Sir Mark Young, the governor of Hong Kong, at 8:30 p.m. on December 25, 1941. I never surrendered. I was wounded and I won an MID, was recommended for the Military Medal for my conduct on the battlefield, and was promoted to command my platoon in action. I served nearly four years in a Japanese prison camp under brutal conditions you could not even imagine. Since the end of the war, I have spent seven months in a military hospital due to severe starvation-induced malnutrition, trying to regain my health and my eyesight. Never once during this ordeal in the service of my country and the Allied cause have I ever complained or shirked my duty. I have never asked for a favour, played politics, or whined about my fate. But now, Captain Burke, I need a favour. I need you, as one soldier to another, to let me have a chance to go to school. I want no guarantees. If I can't start at the junior matriculation level and keep up, then and then only will I admit defeat and go quietly, knowing that I had my chance. I ask for nothing but a single chance to succeed or fail. Furthermore, Captain, if you won't grant me the favour of a chance to go to rehab school, I am going to go to Toronto to see the editor of the *Toronto Star* and, dressed just as I am now, I'm going to tell him my story and your bureaucratic response to it. When I'm finished going over your head, if I have to, your name in the Canadian Army won't be Burke, it will be mud! I can just imagine what the minister of national defence will say about your mistreatment of a veteran of Hong Kong. It will be a political bombshell! Now, Captain, I don't like these tactics, but, by God, sir, I know justice has not been done in my case and I will not back down! The perceived mistreatment of a veteran of Hong Kong will provide the Opposition in the House of Commons just the political scandal they would love to see. The Opposition will love you!"

There was a long silence as Captain Burke gazed up at this solemn, determined young man and considered his options. Finally, he said, "MacDonell, while this is against the rules and my better judgement, I will authorize you to attend the Kitchener rehab school, but only upon the condition that the principal of the school will accept you. I warn you now that he may reject your application, and if he does reject you under the Rehab Act, I cannot overrule him."

And so that is how he solved his problem. He simply passed the buck to the principal of the Kitchener school. He knew that if the principal turned me down, he would be off the hook and the government could blame my rejection on the principal, who was a private citizen.

While Captain Burke had solved his problem, he hadn't solved mine. I saw the game, I saw the danger of rejection was still as real as before, but I wasn't dead yet. There was still a chance — mighty slim it was, but still a chance. Of course, I had no leverage of appealing to politicians with the school principal. He was a non-government volunteer who would soon be back in retirement. No, threats to him would be as empty as a used-up Bren gun magazine. I would need something more powerful to sway the principal. He had no military or government career to protect. He was untouchable in that respect.

My discharge came through on the date promised and I was ordered to report the following Monday morning to Mr. T.E. Merritt, principal of the Kitchener Rehab Institution in Kitchener, Ontario to commence my candidacy for my senior matriculation. This was to be the last class before the closure of the school. I could feel the flames of the educational bridges burning beneath my feet.

Mr. Merritt had been a high-school teacher in Kitchener all his life. He had been a famous principal in Kitchener and a revered inspector of Kitchener-area high schools before he retired from his illustrious career as a much-loved and respected educator of Kitchener's youth. He was six-foot-six, with a shock of white hair and a snowy white beard. He had piercing blue eyes and, at 82 years of age, was mentally as sharp as a tack. He had ruled the Kitchener rehab school since its inception with an iron hand, and he was the master of the students, the teachers, the curriculum, and the school as a whole. Had he been a soldier, he would have at least reached the rank of brigadier. That he was the principal of a school made up of combat veterans didn't faze him one bit. He was the boss and in his presence, you knew it. His school ran like clockwork. There was no nonsense at the Kitchener rehab, and he had a reputation for not suffering fools or malingerers very gladly. I learned all this from a little judicious reconnaissance before my Monday appointment.

I appeared at Mr. Merritt's office in Kitchener on time and still without civilian clothes. I waited in line with other applicants from every service, including a young female lieutenant from the Canadian Women's Army Corps, who had come to present their credentials to Mr. Merritt and to be assigned to their classes, which would commence that day. To say I was nervous was to put it mildly. I knew I was at one of those crossroads of life that was critical. One road led to an opportunity to equip myself for a better and more rewarding life and the other road led to heaven knew what. I also knew that Mr. Merritt held the key to what I thought was my future and that, from his decision, there would be no appeal. I was scared because technically I had a poor argument. I had to depend on his humanitarian instincts, his sense of justice, and his interest in fair play.

Finally, my turn came, my name was called, and I entered the principal's office. His office was the spartanly furnished former office of the military camp commandant. Behind Mr. Merritt on the wall were two large portraits of the King and Queen who stared down unblinking upon their loyal subjects. The office had that barracks smell of floors that had been well-scrubbed with army-issue soap and disinfectant. On his desk before him, Mr. Merritt had my file, which contained my service record and my scanty academic achievement history. After greeting me, he asked me to sit on a straight-backed chair before his desk while he leafed through my file. After a while, he lifted his eyes to mine and said, not unkindly, "There must be a mistake, Mr. MacDonell, we have no classes here that can accommodate you. You see, our classes are for students who have completed two-and-a-half to three years of high school, and your record shows you have no academic high-school standing at all. Your Grade 10 commercial certificate has no standing here. I cannot understand why London sent you to me. They know our courses as well as I do. I'm sorry, but I can't admit you here."

All the while, his blue eyes stared straight into mine and his tone was that of a kindly father explaining the simple facts of life to a somewhat retarded son. There was a long silence as he stared at me with a look partly questioning and partly surprised.

I said, "Mr. Merritt, I know what you say is true and that I present an unusual challenge that the school here is currently unprepared for. I knew before I came that there was no class available at Kitchener that started at the first grade of high school. I came to see you to ask you to let me start at the lowest grade you have. All I want is a chance. If I can't keep up, I will quit, without rancour, knowing I was given a fair chance. I don't want any promises or guarantees. I asked to come to see you personally because of your reputation as one of the finest educators that Kitchener has ever had. I thought that a man such as you who had devoted his life to educating the young would understand my desperate need to get an education. I am willing to devote every waking moment to keeping up with the class if you will just let me try. While my demands upon the rehab system are unusual, sir, so was my service to my country."

Then I told him of our stand against the Japanese at Hong

Kong in 1941, our four years of starvation and slave labour in Japanese prison camps, and about our amazing rescue by the U.S. Marines in northern Japan in the fall of 1945. I pointed out that I had served six years and seven months and had accumulated 79 months of education credits. I finished my speech by saying, "Mr. Merritt, in September of 1939 when you needed me, I stepped forward and I never let you down. Now, Mr. Merritt, I need you to step forward. Please don't let me down!"

He listened intently to the whole speech without revealing his inner thoughts. Then he said, "George, that's quite a story. Your first class will start this afternoon at 2:00 p.m." His simple statement was the end of the conversation. He issued no warnings about not keeping up, he outlined no conditions, nor did he voice any statement of bureaucratic misgivings about his decision.

My heart leaped — I was given the chance I had asked for. At the same time, I realized that he trusted me to live up to my side of the bargain. Now I had even more motivation to succeed, if that were possible. I may have been mistaken but I swear I saw the monarchs smile and the Queen wink as I left the room.

At two o'clock in the afternoon, I attended my first class. It was algebra. If it had been Greek, it wouldn't have been more confusing. At one point halfway through the class, I asked the teacher, who had just been demobilized as a major, why the value of a quantity changed when it was moved across the equal sign. He said, "What was that question?" I repeated it, and as I did I became aware that now every student in the class was staring at me and craning their necks to see who had asked such a silly question.

Then the teacher frowned at me and said that if I didn't know the answer to that question, I shouldn't be in this class. Boy, I thought to myself, going back to school is one long uphill battle. Now the teacher is refusing to teach me. I rose to my feet and said, "But Major, I *am* in this class with the principal's approval and 79 months of earned rehab credits, and I am here to learn.

Perhaps I am mistaken, but I was under the impression that you are here to teach."

The major didn't take very kindly to that reply and several of the other students smiled — but I got my answer.

After the class was over and the other students were filing out of the classroom, the major walked down to me and ordered me to stay behind. After the others had left, he said, "What's the story, Sergeant-Major?" I told him and he said, "You need a tutor, fast."

"I agree," I replied. "Do you know of one?"

He said, "Yes, as a matter of fact, I do."

"Who is it?"

"Me."

"When do we start?"

"Tomorrow morning in this room at 8:00 a.m."

And so began 13 months, 7 days a week, 10 to 12 hours a day of cramming for my college entrance senior matriculation.

After school that day, I answered an ad in the Kitchener paper for a boarder. The people who placed the ad lived three blocks from the school in a brand-new, four-bedroom brick house. Their names were Mr. and Mrs. Schuert and they were kindly Mennonite farmers who had sold their farm and moved into the city to retire. I rented a large bedroom with space for a desk and my books and had both breakfast and dinner with the Schuerts. They were wonderful to me and a never-failing source of encouragement.

I soon made friends with other students who helped me again and again to do my homework, write my assignments, and understand the course material. I had several tutors who were retired teachers who cheerfully came to my residence to tutor me on a regular basis. I just put in the hours it took — no matter how long I had to work. There was no turning back — I had to make it. My teachers did everything they could to help me and somehow, at the end of each month, I scraped through the tests to keep my standing. I soon began to realize that a really highly motivated adult could complete a five-year high-school course in far less time than it took teenagers to master the material. I was thankful for that.

At the end of every two months or so, my mind would seize up and my learning curve drop to zero. When this happened, a couple of my friends and I would declare a weekend holiday and head for the bright lights of Toronto. We booked rooms at the Royal York at $10.00 a night and with our back pay lived like millionaires in Toronto's night spots. We had some hilarious times, blew off large amounts of steam, and forgot about school. But at nine o'clock Monday morning, with terrible hangovers, we were back in our classrooms to continue the struggle.

As month after month and test after test passed, the fear of failure began to decline somewhat, but I can never remember so much anxiety. Even today, I dream sometimes that I am forced to take a test at rehab school for a course I haven't prepared for or studied very well. During this period, I was recalled to the military hospital for a checkup and further tests to ensure that I was free of a horrible parasite I had brought home with me from the Pacific. At the hospital, my doctors, based on my condition, urged me to quit school as the strain was only too evident. I replied by saying, "I'd rather die than quit." It was that simple.

At the end of the 13-month period, the last great hurdle, the days of the final provincial exams, drew near. My teachers gave me sample questions from past final exams and coached me over and over on how to write an answer, both for form and content. For 13 months I had nearly killed myself to prepare for these exams, but was I ready? Finally, the provincial Grade 13 exams were to be written in the last week of May 1947. If I passed, I could enter the University of Toronto as a freshman in September of that same year. If I failed ... I refused to even think about it! At last we sat for the Grade 13 exams, and to my surprise and growing sense of confidence, they weren't so difficult after all.

All classes were then cancelled and the school began to close down forever. I went home to Stratford to stay with my aunt and uncle and my cousins, Helen and David, to nervously await the results. Early in June, we were informed that the exam results would be posted and certificates presented to those who passed at the school at two o'clock on a Thursday afternoon. I took the bus to Kitchener and was on time for the ceremony. There on the bulletin board was my name — I had passed with honours.

Mr. Merritt presented me with my certificate and when he did, my fellow students let out a mighty cheer. The underdog had made it! The ceremony was over by three o'clock. It was a magnificent day in June. The ordeal was over and I clutched my priceless Grade 13 certificate in my hand. As I walked to the Schuerts' house to give them the news, collect my things, and say goodbye, I listened to the birds singing in the tree-lined streets and thought about my mother and how pleased she would be. The short walk from the rehab school to the Schuerts' house in the warm sunshine of that glorious day in June 55 years ago was one of the greatest 15 minutes of my life.

When I arrived at the Schuerts' with my news, Mrs. Schuert put her arms around me and broke into tears, tears of joy at my success and tears of sorrow because she was losing her "boy," for whom she had cared, washed, and cooked and on whose behalf she had, on bended knee, said so many hopeful prayers. I phoned my aunt in Stratford with the good news, and when I returned that night, I received a hero's welcome from my family.

I never forgot the Schuerts. I often wrote them and from time to time visited that wonderful old couple, until they passed away. I also had to say goodbye to a nice girl I had met in Kitchener. It was a tearful goodbye and far more painful than I had ever imagined it would be. I never forgot how much Jeannie and her family had helped me either, and later I sent her a nice present when she was married.

Ten days after the graduation ceremony at the school, my fellow students and I hired the banquet facility at the Walper House in Kitchener's best hotel for a celebration party. This was to be a gala event with champagne and the best dinner their kitchen could prepare. We sent out engraved invitations to Mr. and Mrs. Merritt and the teachers and their wives and on the evening of the great event were pleased to see they all came. After drinks, much champagne, and a wonderful dinner, as the school's longest serving student I was elected, or "joed" as they say in the army, to give a thank-you speech to the principal and the teaching staff. This I did, while highlighting irreverently some of our teachers' foibles and pet sayings, much to the merriment of everyone present, including the teachers mentioned. However, the end of my speech took on a serious tone, and, on behalf of my fellow students, I told the teachers how much we appreciated what they had done for us.

Then Mr. Merritt rose to speak on behalf of the teachers. I wish I had a tape recording of his moving speech. This was perhaps his last public speech and he was prepared. Paraphrasing McCrae's "In Flanders Fields," he told us that he and our teachers had passed to us the "torch" to hold it high, and he enjoined us never to break faith with those of our many comrades who had given their lives for all of us and our freedom. The war was just over and there was no family in Kitchener and no one at that party who had not suffered an intimate loss or knew of one. These words evoked powerful emotions, and each of us flashed back to images of fields of white crosses "row on row" that marked "their" place. He said as teachers they had passed on to us what their generation believed and held dear and that they had confidence they would be proud of us. He said they all felt it had been a great joy and a privilege to be our teachers, and they wished us happiness, good luck, and Godspeed. We then sang "Auld Lang Syne" and there wasn't a dry eye in the room.

What a fine old man he was and how lucky we had been to have known him!

Now, in June of 1947, another chapter had come to an end. I looked forward, as a bona fide 25-year-old high-school graduate, to the exciting new world of higher education and the university. The rehab experience taught me a lesson. I learned that academic success is more a product of character, hard work, and careful preparation than it is of anything else. Other things being equal, success in life and high marks in school seemed to go to those who work. As in the fable of the tortoise and the hare, the steady, persistent, hard-working tortoise may be slower and less flamboyant, but it's amazing how far hard work and determination will take you. It was a comfort to me (the tortoise) to learn the race doesn't always go to the swift.

I got a job for the summer on the CNR as a clerk for a big gang of labourers who were laying and welding new track from Stratford to London. I worked for the foreman of the gang, lived in a mobile bunkhouse, ate enormous cookhouse meals, and saved every penny I earned. Not yet fit for heavy work, my job was to plan the work assignments and to see to it that the rails, oxygen cylinders, welding supplies, food, water, fuel, and everything else were on hand to keep the work flowing smoothly. I got the job because I had a Grade 13 high-school diploma. I could see and reap the benefits of my new educational status within a couple of weeks of graduation.

I also went to Toronto to the university on a reconnaissance mission. I went to see the registrar and applied to do a three-year B.A. in two years. "Just give me a chance," I said. I learned that, located right on the campus, there was a men's residence called 73 St. George Street. This residence was for out-of-town scholarship students and would be a wonderful place to live if I were accepted. I learned that 73 St. George Street was for elite out-of-town scholars who had won scholarships to University College.

This residence was under the supervision of the former adjutant of the Toronto Scottish who was now the dean of men at University College. His name was Claude Bissell and he later became a well-known president of the University of Toronto. I went to see him and asked to be billeted at 73 St. George Street. He said, "No, no, you wouldn't want to be in a residence full of inexperienced academic whiz kids; you want to be at Holwood Hall with the other veterans."

"No, no," I said, "Captain Bissell, I want to be as far away as I can from that gang of partying, beer-drinking veterans, fighting World War II all over again, ad infinitum. I'll never get any work done there. I am a serious student who just did five years of high school in 13 months and I want to be surrounded by scholars. I want to get my B.A. in two years. I want peace and quiet and to be with motivated scholarship students. Besides, wouldn't it be a good idea to have at least one service veteran in with these kids?"

Bissell laughed and said, "Well, there's no law that says you can't live at 73 St. George Street. I'll see what I can do."

I knew that as he was a just-demobilized captain of the Canadian Corps of Infantry and the ex-adjutant of the Toronto Scottish, I had a good chance. Then he invited me to his residence on the campus for tea and to meet his charming Scottish wife, whom he had recently married. What a lovely lady! During tea, we swapped stories and fought the war all over again and had a wonderful time telling each other of our different wartime experiences.

True to his word, within a couple of weeks I received in the mail permission to take up residence at 73 St. George Street. Once again, Lady Luck had played a hand, but as it turned out, I wasn't the only veteran at 73 St. George Street. There was another. He was Wing Commander Campbell of the RCAF and we became close friends. While I was at the university, I asked at the registrar's office for a list of subjects I would have to take as a first-year student in the fall and a list of the books that had been required reading for these courses in the academic year just completed. Armed with this list, I bought some of the most important works at the university book store to take back to the job on the railway. I thought if I was going to pass three years in two, I'd better be prepared. As I look back, I can see I must have been just a bit too anxious and, to my railway friends, a bit of a nut! I can guarantee that I was the only railroad worker that summer in Ontario who, by the light of a kerosene lamp after supper, was busy reading Chaucer's *Canterbury Tales* in a mobile bunkhouse.

Chapter Ten

The Transition

I could hardly wait for the summer of 1947 to pass. I had just earned my senior matriculation at rehab school. I had been accepted to study at University College at the University of Toronto and had also been confirmed as a resident member of the men's residence on the campus at 73 St. George Street.

The summer of 1947 was a summer of remarkably good weather, and it was a very exciting time for Canadians as well. The country was busily engaged in the process of adjusting from the discipline and the focused, single-minded national effort to win the war to a less structured, more diverse, and relaxed civilian economy. Consumer goods such as automobiles, clothing, and refrigerators, though still in short supply, began to appear in dealers' stores across the nation. Food and gasoline rationing disappeared and restricted items such as sugar and butter became available in the grocery stores. Ration cards were no longer necessary. Factories that had produced every kind of war material, from tanks and bombers to naval five-inch shells, were slowly changing over and beginning to produce refrigerators, vacuum cleaners, electric stoves, and a wide variety of consumer hardware. It had been a long war with many shortages for Canadian civilians, and there was an enormous pent-up demand for a multitude of consumer goods.

It was an exciting time for another reason. By now, all of Canada's armed forces had returned from the far corners of the earth and were urgently trying to return to old jobs and new opportunities for employment in the post-war Canadian economy. It was also an exciting time because, during the war, Canadians had accomplished things that no one before the war had dreamed we were capable of. Canadians were bursting with pride and understandably had hopes, dreams, and high expectations for themselves and our country. We were no longer the unimportant, largely rural producers of natural resources such as wheat, minerals, and lumber up in the bush somewhere in the wilderness in North America above the 49th parallel. Now Canada was on the map as a real player in the world of commerce and had a strong and audible voice in international politics. Lester Pearson and his Canadian colleagues in External Affairs were helping to shape the United Nations in the post-war world. This was big-league stuff. We had earned a place at the table of international affairs.

We now had a new dimension to our economy. We had a burgeoning manufacturing sector and a growing "big steel" industry to support it. The sky was the limit and foreign dignitaries, including Winston Churchill, agreed with us that "the 20th century belonged to Canada."

In the middle of this hustle and bustle and optimism about the future, I was free, had nearly $3,000 back pay in the bank, and was going to realize my dream of going to university. Somehow I had survived the battles, the slave labour, and the prison camps and now my whole life stretched before me, to do with what I would and what I could. But things were not quite so simple or quite so easy as they appeared on the surface. Yes, it was true that I was home, physically free, and my health was beginning to improve, but I wasn't as free or untroubled as I might have appeared on the surface. I found I could not forget what had happened in the last four years, and I especially could not forget the fate of my comrades who had not returned from Hong Kong and Japan. These memories continued to disturb and trouble me.

On several occasions, I was asked to visit the mothers and fathers of those in my company or regiment who had not returned. After these visits, I would become deeply depressed. One such visit was to the mother of Sergeant David Lumb, who had died of starvation and amoebic dysentery in captivity as a PoW in Hong Kong in the spring of 1942. During the war, David's father had passed away and now Mrs. Lumb was alone, having lost both her husband and her only son. Mrs. Lumb was grief-stricken and could not bring herself to believe that her only son was dead and buried thousands of miles away, somewhere in a foreign land in alien soil. She refused to accept the army's report of his death and its circumstances, and so, since I had known Sergeant Lumb, I was asked to go and see her.

One beautiful June day, I went to London to visit Mrs. Lumb in her little suburban home. While David Lumb had not been in my company, we became friends as PoWs. Mrs. Lumb was very grateful that I had come to see her and confided in me that she could not believe her handsome young son was dead. I tried to convince her that he had died in North Point prison camp and that I had attended his funeral. I tried to console her. It was a terrible experience for both of us. I had never seen such grief.

It was through these sorrowful meetings that I began to really understand the awful consequences of war and to feel deeply, to the core of my being, the suffering of the mothers and fathers, the brothers and sisters, the wives and sweethearts who had lost a loved one. I was deeply depressed after this meeting with Mrs. Lumb. Having survived the battle, I had no answer as to "why" David had to die. The memory of that sad meeting and the emotions of sorrow and pity that it aroused in me are branded on my memory to this day.

During the years that followed, I never shook off the sad memories of the past, and very seldom have I lived through a day in the last 60 years entirely free of the tragedy of Hong Kong and the seemingly unnecessary deaths of so many of those young men. Again and again, I have lived through the horror of those four years in my dreams. These dreams persist even to this day and the theme is always the same. In my dreams, I learn that we prisoners in Japan will never be allowed to go free or see our families and Canada again. Even though the war is over, we will remain forever in Japan as slave labourers and as prisoners of the Japanese.

I tried to forget by avoiding anything to do with the Hong Kong Veterans Association, and while, at the time, I thought it helped, it probably didn't. There was really no one I could talk to except my wife, and I tried to avoid burdening her, so I was alone with my inner feelings. It was decades before I began to realize that I had developed a deep-seated unconscious feeling of guilt because so many had died and I had lived. And so, for longer than I care to admit, my joy in my wife and children and in my career was marred by these awful recurring feelings of guilt at my survival and my good fortune.

Finally, I decided that it would be a good thing for the children and the grandchildren of my Hong Kong comrades, and my own children, if I wrote an eyewitness account to record, just as I saw it, what happened in December of 1941 at Hong Kong — so long ago. I wanted to record for all Canadians and for posterity the little-known and almost completely forgotten story of the courage and loyalty of that small force of Canadians who, when faced with their moment of truth, never flinched, never failed their country or each other, and never surrendered to the enemy. Only when I began to write and once again to contact and talk to my surviving veteran colleagues from Hong Kong did I begin to find release from the depression and feelings of guilt that had plagued me for so long. I learned that while we had each reacted in different ways, none of us had escaped the emotional burden of our experience in the Far East. In these discussions, it was comforting to learn that I was not alone.

At last, the great day in September of 1947 came. It was time to say goodbye to my railway construction crew friends and take the train to Toronto and my new home at 73 St. George Street and to prepare for commencement day at University College.

I was given a comfortable room overlooking the campus at the university men's residence and soon settled into the academic atmosphere of that venerable old mansion that had seen so many generations of eager young students come and go. I learned we were to eat our meals in the main hall at Hart House, at a special table reserved for the members of 73 St. George Street. I was living in style on the campus, surrounded by scholarship students. Just what I had hoped for. There were 30 male students at 73 St. George Street, and I often think back to the wonderful times we had together. Of course, the freshmen, at age 19, were in awe of an old man like me who, at age 25, had served nearly seven years in the Canadian Army in World War II and who, from time to time, was invited to take tea with Dean Bissell and his wife.

The first week after commencement was the time for the initiation ceremonies of the freshmen. It had become a long-standing tradition at the residence that the seniors put the freshmen through a series of mildly sadistic, painful, and very humiliating initiation exercises that lasted about a week. The president of the house called for a general meeting one day after supper of all house members. He announced the names, including mine, of the freshman victims of the house who were to appear the following night at eight o'clock for the first initiation rites on the back campus. After he was finished, I rose and said, "Mr. President, while I understand the house tradition of initiating freshmen, there will be one freshman who will *not* be present tomorrow evening at eight o'clock on the back campus, and that person will be me. You see, gentlemen, I have already been initiated at Wolseley Barracks in London, Ontario, in 1940, and my initiation lasted not one week, but nine months. Under the circumstances, I think you will agree that I have already undergone my initiation, and because of that, I think you will also agree I should not be required to go through another."

My comments were regarded as a motion from the floor, which was debated, put to a vote, and decided in my favour. Wing Commander Campbell was granted the same exemption.

I loved the university and everything about it. I was elected president of my first-year class of 1947–48 at University College. This position entitled me to sit on the university students' council. As a council member, I became involved in university politics. The president of the university at that time was Sidney Smith. It wasn't long before I was before the president, with other members of the council, in his panelled office arguing the case to allow the Communist "Red Dean" Howlett of Canterbury, England, to speak to the student body. This was great fun and no doubt a big pain to President Smith. After several meetings with him, he reversed his decision to bar the Red Dean and agreed to allow the student council to extend an invitation to him to come to Toronto, at his own expense, to address the varsity students in Convocation Hall. None of us were converted to communism.

In the first week after convocation, I had the greatest stroke of luck of my entire life when I met the person who was to become my wife, my wonderful partner, and my best friend for life. A friend of mine named Bill Stuart, from Guelph, invited me to join him at a get-acquainted dance staged for freshmen at University College, sponsored by the students' council. When we got to the dance, it was crowded with young people in their freshman year attending their first social event at the university. It didn't take us long to become aware of an especially beautiful young woman who, with a female friend, was surrounded by a group of young men. Eventually, we elbowed our way through the throng and introduced ourselves. I was instantly smitten! She was beautiful and glowed with an aura of warmth and goodness that I found deeply attractive. However, she wasn't a freshman; she was a lecturer in the Department of Sociology and was an M.A. graduate from McMaster University. She was 21 and had been born in Burma where her father was a famous Baptist missionary. Her name was Margaret Telford and, from that moment on, I began to plot a way to change her last name to MacDonell.

However, I was not alone in my interest. There were other young men with exactly the same idea. At one point when she barely knew of me, I handed in to my professor a review of a book on Japan written by Margaret Mead, the famous American anthropologist. At the time, I didn't know Margaret was his assistant, responsible for marking our papers. When the book review was returned, it was graded with a B. I regarded a B as an affront. Was I not an authority on Japan? After all, I had lived there for four years. How dare they give me a B?

In the next "spare" period, I went to the professor's office to complain. His secretary said he was out but I could speak to his assistant, Miss Margaret Telford, about my marks. I went to Margaret's office to be greeted with her smile and her question if she could be of help.

Holding up my paper, I said, "I came to see about my grade on this Margaret Mead book report. My paper was graded B and I do not get Bs! I want to know who graded this paper a B and why."

Margaret looked at me and calmly said, "Well, Mr. MacDonell, I marked your paper and I graded it a B and as far as I am concerned, it will stay a B." But, with another smile, she said, "I am pleased you take your work and your marks so seriously, and I will take up your complaint with the professor."

At her words and her smile, the wind of indignation died in my sails, and as I crept out of the building, I cursed myself as a fool for such a silly, self-righteous speech in front of that beautiful, sophisticated girl. I learned after we were married that, true to her word, she did go to see the professor and told him that, because she was becoming emotionally involved with a student named George MacDonell, she preferred not to grade any more of his work.

I plunged into my studies and revelled in the world of ideas I found at the university. I quickly made friends with my veteran classmates and we had a wonderful time together as we debated how to save the world. As I look back on that period, I remember that not only were we very idealistic but we were convinced that "big government" was the solution to society's problems and we were very anxious to take part in the creation of a better world. We had been impressed by what the wartime government of Canada had been able to accomplish. We saw how the Canadian Army and the other services, ruled from the top, became a powerful, disciplined, and effective instrument of Canada's Parliament and our foreign policy. We reasoned that, if centralized power in the hands of a few dependent upon the loyalty and obedience of the many could defeat Germany and Japan, it could easily solve any of our current social problems such as poverty, illiteracy, and unemployment. As ex-servicemen and -women, we didn't have to be convinced of the efficacy of socialized medicine as we had been living under a highly organized and very effective form of military socialized medicine in the services for years. We realized there was a vast difference between a military government and a free democratic civilian society. We understood there was no place in post-war Canada for totalitarianism, but we nonetheless felt strongly that big government could be the answer to our social problems.

At that time, as today, there was little support for conservative thought or ideas at the university. In our zeal for social reform and to make Canada and the world a better and more humane place, many of us became what today would be called left-wingers. We devoured the famous Beveridge Report, which was to become one of the foundations of the British socialist movement, and were deeply impressed by its socialist blueprint for a better society.

I became interested in, and a supporter of, government-built and -subsidized social-housing projects for the city's poor and underprivileged. While at the university, I worked as a graduate student assistant to Professor Allan Rose of the School of Social Work. Dr. Rose was a pioneer in social housing and his work in this field finally led to the creation of the post-war Alexander Park Housing Project and others in downtown Toronto. At that time, full of goodwill and enthusiasm for social housing, we did not foresee the eventual negative consequences of these publicly funded housing projects and the crime and social stigma they seemed to foster in their residents. Our sense of social justice and our desire for social reform often blinded us to the difference between how people actually behave and how we thought they "should" behave. We were, no doubt, well-meaning, but naive. We had seen what a mess the world was in, and we were in a hurry to change it for the better. This all made for stirring debates in the King Cole Room bar across the street at the Park Plaza, in the classrooms, in the men's residence, and at the dinner table at Hart House.

I gained my B.A. in two years and, wearing cap and gown and accompanied by my fiancée, Margaret Telford, received my Bachelor of Arts certificate one beautiful June day at Convocation Hall with my classmates. Yes, this hard-working tortoise graduated with straight As. Oh, what a day it was! In little more than three years, I had graduated from high school and had a B.A. What a wonderful opportunity my country had provided for me and my veteran friends. Now it was on to graduate school to obtain an M.A.

That summer, I took a summer job as the guardian of the grandchildren of Mrs. W.L. Matthews at her summer estate at Roches Point on Lake Simcoe. Her son was the Canadian ambassador to Washington and Mrs. Matthews had agreed to look after her four grandchildren for the summer. I was asked by the warden of Hart House to apply for the job as he had been asked by Mrs. Matthews to recommend a student. I didn't want the job but agreed as a favour to him to be interviewed by Mrs. Matthews. I went to her mansion in Forest Hill and when asked about my salary, I quoted a figure I knew was far too high. When I voiced my salary requirements, she paused and asked me to repeat my salary terms, as if she couldn't believe her ears. When I repeated them without blushing, she smiled and said, "Agreed. Sidney, my chauffeur, will pick up your things tomorrow and you can move in here until the children arrive from Washington next week."

The next thing I knew, I was out on the street with a summer job at a wonderful salary I had never expected to get. I couldn't go back and admit I was a fraud! And so the very next day, chauffeured by Sidney, I went to live in Mrs. Matthews's home, not as a servant, she told me, but as the guardian of her grandchildren. That meant I had all my meals with her and the children and I was a kind of father substitute for the summer.

The Roches Point summer home was another mansion, beautifully sited on acres of land fronting on Lake Simcoe. There were three servants, a cook and two maids, Sidney the chauffeur, and a gardener. My word was law as far as the safety of the children was concerned at Roches Point, and I never let those kids out of my sight or out of my mind for even a moment. When my first payday came, Mrs. Matthews told me she was saving my salary until the end of my employment period when it would be paid in full. In the meantime, she said, giving me an envelope full of cash, "This is your expense money."

"Expense money?" I said. "We didn't discuss expense money."

Emphatically, she said, "Well, I must have forgotten to mention it, but while you're here, you will be receiving expense money every week."

That was the end of that discussion!

Again, Lady Luck dealt me a lucky break. I could save my entire summer earnings, but that wasn't the only benefit I was to receive. Mrs. Matthews was a widow and the sister of Sir William Mulock, the world-famous physician. She was immensely wealthy, highly educated, and a simply wonderful human being. After dinner and after the children were tucked into bed, Mrs. Matthews and I would sit together on the verandah and talk. Rather, she would talk and I would listen. What an experience for me to listen to her life story, to hear of her travels and the people she had met and the experiences of this gifted woman. When she was a girl, her father invited Sir Winston Churchill to stay with them when he was on a speaking tour of North America. She said her father thought Winston a "stuffed shirt" because he always insisted on "dressing" for dinner. She thought he was wonderful! She was a personal friend of Lester Pearson and the "who's who" of that period. What an odd couple we were — the naive, penniless, 25-year-old soldier-student and the wealthy, cultured, erudite Mrs. Matthews. What a wonderful education for me!

For her birthday, I gave her a copy of a biography of Joseph Stalin. She asked, "Why Joseph Stalin?" and she laughed when I replied, "I gave you that book because, as far as I can see, he's the only famous person you don't know."

After my 16 weeks were up and we said goodbye, our friendship continued, and over the subsequent years she invited Margaret and me and our children to her home many times, until she passed away.

In September of that year, Margaret and I were married and went to live in an attic on Spadina Road, just north of St. Clair Avenue. The attic had a bedroom, a sitting room, and a bathroom, but no kitchen, so we set up two hot plates on orange crates in the hallway and washed our dishes in the bathtub. Margaret got a job as an assistant to Dr. Faludi, the famous town planner, which earned her $100 per month. As a veteran student, I earned $60 and so we had a combined income of $160 per month. We were poor but so were all our friends, and we were very happy. We lacked for nothing and looked forward to the day we could buy a house and have children.

I did well at graduate school where, again, hard work was the essential ingredient for recognition, and because I was serious about my work, I got to know my outstanding professors, including such academics as Dr. Albert Rose, S.J. Clark, Dr. Harold Innes, and Professor Bladen, the author of the Canada/U.S. Auto Pact. Their influence on me was enormous. My wife,

Margaret, was an academic star and was of great help during this period as well.

One day, the phone rang in the attic. The caller asked me if my name was G.S. MacDonell. When I replied that, yes, indeed, I was, her next question was, "And are you the author of an article or treatise entitled 'A Content Analysis of Management-Labour Communications Programs'?"

Again, the answer was, "Yes, I am." By now, I began to feel somewhat apprehensive about what was coming next. At this point, I said to my somewhat haughty sounding caller, "Do you mind telling me why you are asking these questions?"

She replied, "Well, apparently your paper had something to say about Canadian General Electric and I have been asked by Mr. H.M. Turner, the President of CGE, to call you to make an appointment to see him here at head office, 212 King Street West, next Wednesday morning at nine o'clock."

I noticed she didn't ask me if I was agreeable to the meeting; she had issued a summons. Then it struck me like a ton of bricks. My heart sank — I had written and handed in as a term paper to my professor of labour relations a content analysis of two years of the contents of CGE's and the United Electrical Workers union's newspapers. The recipients of these communications were the same people — the workers of CGE. My analysis and conclusions pointed out, confidentially I thought, to my professor in my paper that CGE was losing the propaganda war for the support of its employees by a country mile and that the Communist UEW union newspaper was winning it. I was not gentle in my descriptions of CGE's alleged failures. My blunt criticisms of the big corporation impressed my professor, who laughed and rewarded me with an A, but now I thought, what have I done? Had I committed libel? Did I need a lawyer to defend me? Who had leaked the paper? Had I compromised the university?

I headed for my professor's office to ask him how my paper had come into the hands of the president of CGE. He confessed that he, in fact, had given the paper to Mr. Turner, as he thought it might be "good for him." He didn't tell me they had been close friends for years and that Turner was a big contributor to the university.

I was certainly apprehensive when my appointment with CGE's president came due. I saw no good coming home from this meeting. When I was ushered into his office, he asked me to sit down and tossed my paper across the desk to me. "Did you write that paper?" he asked.

"Yes, sir," I replied.

"Do you believe what you wrote?"

"Yes, sir," I gulped.

"So do I," he said. "Unfortunately, what you said about our communication program is all too true."

Well, you could have knocked me over with a feather. What I thought was going to be a serious tongue-lashing and maybe a removal of my government scholarship turned out to be my first offer of a job.

"But sir," I said, "I won't finish my M.A. for nearly two years at the earliest."

"Oh," he said, "I've fixed that with the registrar at the university. You can get your M.A. by working for me in the morning and going to school in the afternoon until you have earned the needed credits for your degree."

"What would I do at CGE?" I asked.

He said I'd go to work in the industrial relations department of the company, starting the next Monday morning. "Now," he said, "We will start you off at $40 per week."

"Forty dollars a week?" I gasped in surprise at such a sum.

He paused and then said, "All right, damn it, $50 a week!"

By this time, I was in shock. Fifty dollars a week! I remember getting up, shaking his outstretched hand, and mumbling thank you or something and staggering out onto King Street to catch the streetcar home to tell Margaret that we were rich! No more attics without a kitchen. We had just gone from my salary of $15 a week to $50 a week and a job with one of Canada's best-known large companies to boot and all over a term paper. Alleluia! Apparently, my luck as a civilian was to take a turn for the better.

And so, with General Electric I began a business career that lasted for 32 years, until my retirement on January 1, 1990. I stayed with Canadian General Electric for the first 20 years and subsequently held a series of executive positions in other companies. I retired in 1981.

A few months after my retirement, I joined the Government of Ontario in July of 1982 on a six-month contract in the Trade Division of the Ministry of Industry, Trade, and Technology, under Deputy Minister Bernard Ostry. This was another lucky break as he was a highly experienced civil servant with a distinguished record in Ottawa before he came to Queen's Park in Ontario. At that time, our minister was the forceful and energetic Gordon Walker from London, Ontario. Ostry was a strong supporter of me and my ideas and when he passed on to another assignment in the government, Premier Bill Davis appointed me deputy minister of that ministry. As our mission was to promote trade, increase exports to foreign markets, and encourage industrial development, this assignment was the most rewarding and enjoyable of my life. In this position, I had the opportunity to know and serve under three premiers of Ontario and three ministers, including Premiers Davis, Peterson, and Miller, and Ministers Walker, Brandt, and O'Neil. One of the important goals of our ministry during that period was to double Ontario's export sales, from $30 billion to $60 billion annually. I served in the Government of Ontario for five years and when I retired, Ontario companies' export sales reached $61 million in that year, creating tens of thousands of new jobs. In 1990, I retired again — this time for good.

This year, 2002, will mark the 61st anniversary of the Battle of Hong Kong. As I look back, on a personal basis, I have no regrets. If the situation was the same today and our country and our way of life were threatened as they were in 1939, I would volunteer to go through it all again.

I hope *One Soldier's Story* will contribute to an understanding of what happened at Hong Kong and in Japanese prison camps and will be a lasting tribute to the character of the men of the Royal Rifles and the Winnipeg Grenadiers who fought there for Canada, so far away and so long ago. I believe that if those who failed to return from Hong Kong and the Japanese prison camps and who gave their lives could speak to us today, they would agree that if we cherish our freedom, we must have the courage to defend it.

Unfortunately, as the events of September 11, 2001, attest, the world is not yet free of those who do not share, or respect, our ideas or our values, and it is still a dangerous place, especially for the unprepared and the unwary. I hope, therefore, that as well as a recounting of the unbreakable spirit and sacrifice of the Canadians at Hong Kong, *One Soldier's Story* will also be a reminder, especially to the young people of Canada, that if we wish to enjoy our freedom in this wonderful country of ours, we must always be prepared to defend it.

Epilogue

Not enough good can be said about our American allies. Instead of ignoring our plight and leaving us unaided to escape from our camp in northern Japan if we could, they left no stone unturned to find, supply, protect, and rescue us. Imagine the cost and effort to supply us from their air bases in the faraway Mariana Islands alone, from which the return flight to Japan took a giant 6-engine B29 bomber 16 hours to complete. Their kindness and generosity and the care of our sick could not have been exceeded. No naval fleet, hospital ship, airplane, marines' or pilots' lives, or taxpayers' money was too much to spend or put at risk for us. I never see the Stars and Stripes waving in the breeze or hear the sound of the Star Spangled Banner but that I remember the kindness of our American friends.

The decision to send C Force to Hong Kong was a tragic mistake made by a badly informed and badly advised Cabinet who were not experienced in the decisions of war. The mental and physical trauma experienced by those who survived has been widespread and severe. Unemployability, alcoholism, chronic illness, blindness, and shortened lives have been the consequences, both mental and physical, of prolonged savagery, malnutrition, and forced labour. Progressively, as the Canadian government began to understand the survivors' plights, special legislation has been passed to increase the levels of both care and pensions for the veterans and their surviving widows.

For many years, the government of Japan refused to honour a long-standing Hong Kong veterans' claim for compensation for being forced to work as slave labour while under Japanese control. The War Amps of Canada spearheaded a successful campaign to emphasize the justice and validity of this demand for compensation and in December of 1998 the Canadian federal government paid the disputed claim. The payment amounted to $24,000 ($18 per day) and was paid to surviving Hong Kong veterans and, more importantly, to the surviving widows of veterans who were deceased.

While there are now very few Hong Kong veterans left, this last generous act was nonetheless clear proof of the sympathy, understanding, and kindness of the Canadian people. Canadians have not forgotten the veterans of Hong Kong or their ordeal of nearly 60 years ago.

Bibliography

Banfill, Dr. Stanley, Diary. Unpublished.

Dower, John W., *Embracing Defeat: Japan in the Wake of World War II*. (New York: W. Norton & Company, 1999.)

Forsyth, Tom, Diary. Unpublished.

Frank, Richard B., *Downfall: The End of the Imperial Japanese Empire*. (New York: Random House, 1999.)

Marston, G.C., Diary. Unpublished.

McIntosh, David, *Hell on Earth: Aging Faster, Dying Soon: Canadian Prisoners of the Japanese During World War II*. (Toronto: McGraw-Hill Ryerson Ltd., 1997.)

Penny, Arthur G, *Royal Rifles of Canada: Able and Willing since 1962, A Short History.* (Quebec City: Sinp, 1962.)

Ross, Lance. Diary. Unpublished.

Stacey, C.P., *Official History of the Canadian Army in the Second World War: Volume I Six Years of War: The Army in Canada, Britain and the Pacific* (Queen's Printer, Ottawa, ON 1960)

Vincent, Carl, *No Reason Why: The Canadian Hong Kong Tragedy.* (Stittsville, Ont.: Canada's Wings Inc., 1981.)